COOKING WITHOUT RECIPES

a mother's journey toward

a whole, natural life

WRITTEN BY ELIZA ELLER
ILLUSTRATED BY MIRRA KOHLMOOS

dedicated to my children who have
given me much motivation, sweet love
and many good times:

the elders John Emrys, Katherine, Jane, Gregory,
the middles Alexander, Lauden, Aaron, Connor,
James and Liam,

and the little girls Ellen, Rosalie and Juliet

© 2016 by eliza eller

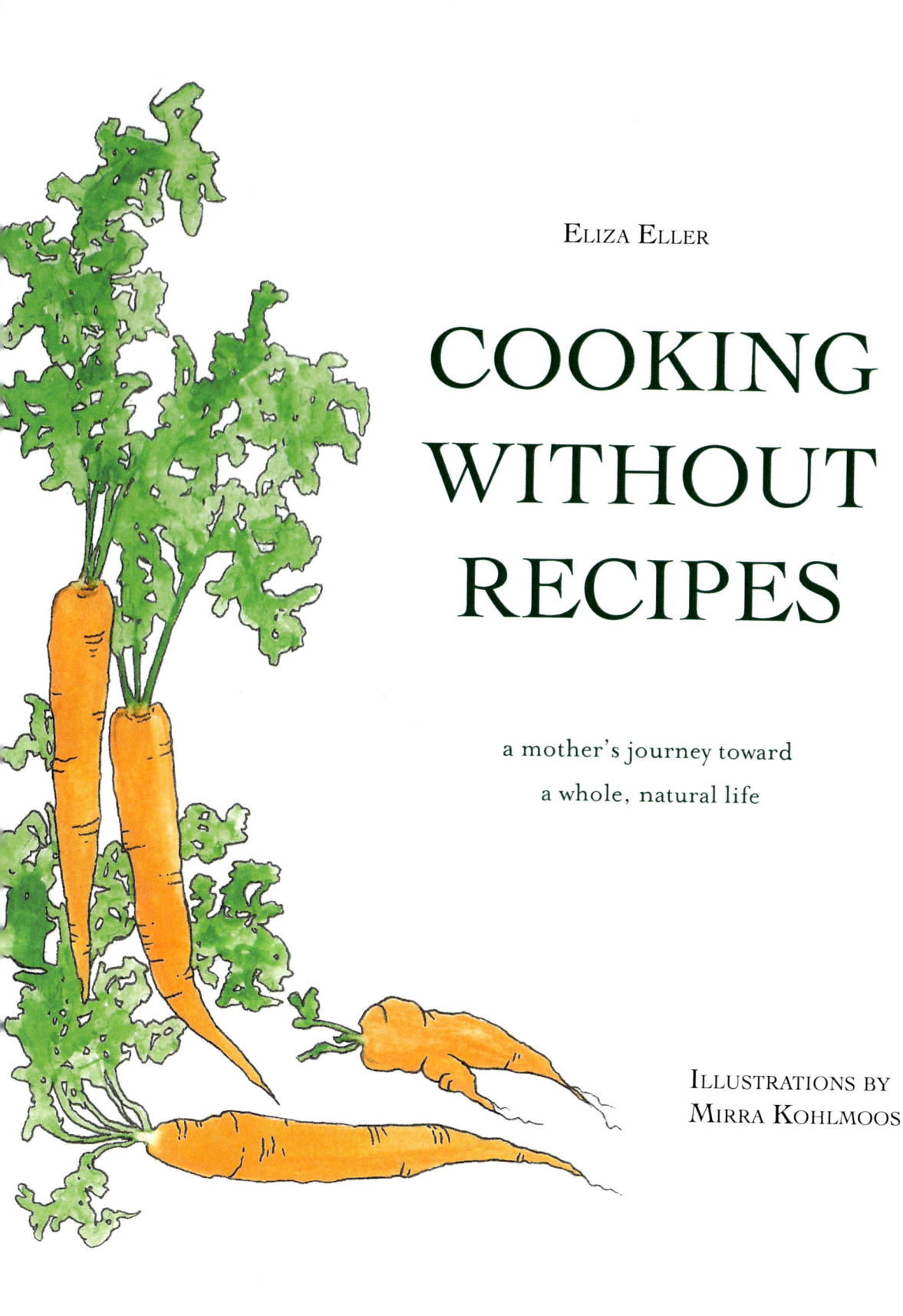

Eliza Eller

COOKING WITHOUT RECIPES

a mother's journey toward

a whole, natural life

Illustrations by
Mirra Kohlmoos

TABLE OF CONTENTS

FORWARD by phiya kushi / 1

PROLOGUE / 3

BEGINNINGS / 6

~ introducing myself / 7
~ introducing Ionia / 9
~ life as we know it / 11
~ food as energy / 12

INGREDIENTS / 14

~ the broader picture / 15
~ let's play is it animal, plant or mineral? / 16
~ the cultural context: why do we eat what we eat? / 18
~ basics of variety & balance / 19
~ continuum of energies / 29

FAMILY / 30

~ from womb to weaning / 31
~ little people / 45
~ finding company and sourcing ingredients / 48
~ illness, injury and home remedies / 51

COOKING / 58

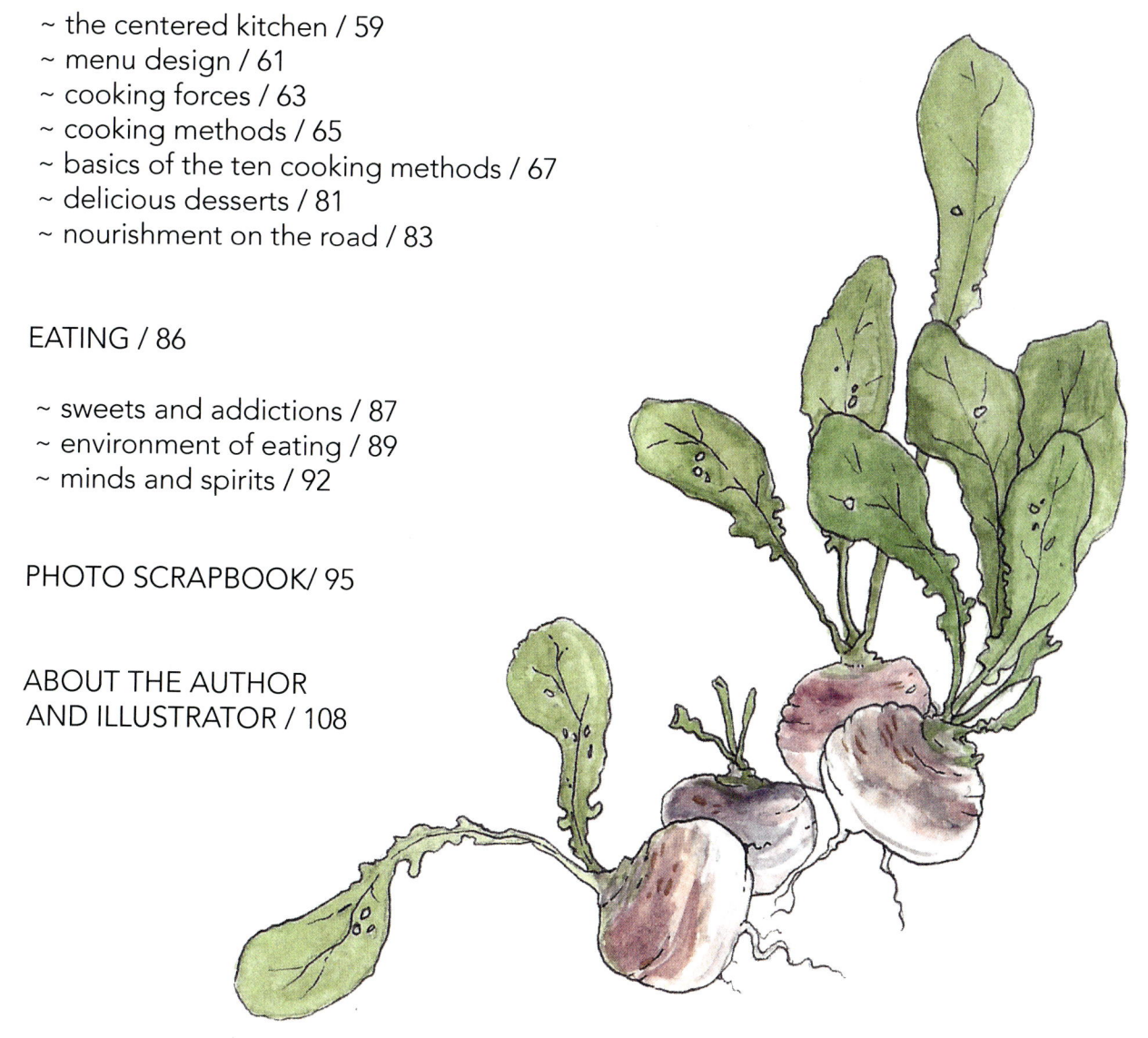

~ the centered kitchen / 59
~ menu design / 61
~ cooking forces / 63
~ cooking methods / 65
~ basics of the ten cooking methods / 67
~ delicious desserts / 81
~ nourishment on the road / 83

EATING / 86

~ sweets and addictions / 87
~ environment of eating / 89
~ minds and spirits / 92

PHOTO SCRAPBOOK / 95

ABOUT THE AUTHOR
AND ILLUSTRATOR / 108

FORWARD

As third son of Michio and Aveline Kushi, I grew up at the center of a philosophical and biological food revolution that continues to evolve and grow today. The Boston macrobiotic community that my parents established in the late 60s thrived through the 70s, 80s and 90s, and gave birth to numerous movements of social change that continue to spread around the world today. These include the development of the organic and natural foods industry, the development of preventive and alternative medicine, and the overall rise in awareness of the direct impact that changes in our food, diet and lifestyles have on our health, environment and happiness.

The inspiration for these threads of change was a grand vision and philosophy of a holistic understanding of the universe based on a way of eating and living in closer harmony with nature, better known as "macrobiotics." Every week my father gave lectures, and my mother taught cooking classes, that respectively outlined this grand vision and practical way of living. Key to this vision was the understanding and belief that we can change ourselves and our world for the better, by changing what we eat, and how we live.

My parents opened up their home to their students, and over time thousands of individuals graced our home and actively joined this peaceful biological revolution. Our home kitchen became center stage, where individuals learned how to prepare whole grains, beans, fresh vegetables and other foods their grandparents used to make, but have since been lost in the rush for processed, industrial, convenient foods. The ongoing classes led to natural food stores, restaurants, food companies and wholesalers, as well books, magazines and teaching centers around the world. As a result, I now have thousands of friends in every country involved in a variety of activities from environmental activism, integrative healthcare, organic food and agriculture industry, macrobiotic education and, of course, teaching cooking with whole natural ingredients.

Among those who studied early on with my parents were Eliza Eller and her family. Unlike many who were inspired to start new ventures and businesses, Eliza and her family went in a different direction. My father had once said that there were two ways in which a person can change the world... One was to focus on being very socially active and inspire many people, and the other was to have many children. Eliza chose the latter and pursued a dream of creating a community based on the vision and philosophy laid out by my parents. She chose the road less travelled.

While many other friends found a variety of success pursing macrobiotic business and activities over the years, Eliza, with her family, and a small group of close friends and their families, took on the more difficult challenge of changing the world by growing their families. With a tremendous amount of courage, they dove head first into the challenge, exploring and defining what it means to live collectively and raise their children with macrobiotic principles and free from the distractions of the modern world. They embraced macrobiotic values of simplicity, whole foods and living in harmony with nature, and, in doing so, faced many challenges, including living in tipis year-round through harsh Alaskan winters. Unfettered, they persevered, and after 35 years their small community, which they named "Ionia", continues to thrive today with a handful of new (and very healthy) third generation babies born recently!

The challenges faced, and lessons Eliza learned over the years, involved exploring all aspects of daily macrobiotic communal living that, as far as I am aware, are not found anywhere else. They range from home birthing, nursing, home schooling, growing foods, cooking, traditional food processing, building natural homes, and overcoming a variety of challenges and difficulties presented by a communal macrobiotic life. "Cooking Without Recipes" is only the tip of an iceberg of a wealth of knowledge acquired by Eliza that can best be described as exploring a macrobiotic life without conformity and compromise, and free from the rules and constraints of the modern world.

I sincerely hope you enjoy this book, and that it inspires you to find your own spirit of adventure to explore the uncharted territories of creating your own natural lifestyle and community toward a more peaceful, healthier and happier world.

Thank you,
Phiya Kushi
October 5, 2015

PROLOGUE

In my earliest memory, I am skipping down a dusty dirt lane, watching the baby goats kicking and bleating amongst grey green hillside. The tangy taste of lemon grass tickles my lips, and the goats run away over the crest of the hill, and I run back, through the open kitchen door, to a wooden chair, painted blue. I dig into a bowl of steaming oats, swimming in honey and raw milk. Golden sunshine rays streak across the kitchen, and honey drips down my spoon, and my mother is near. These scenes are as images from a dream, and I have no context nor time for them. I think they are memories of Ojai, California, in 1966 when I was two years old, where my mother visited for a few days when she was leaving my father. As I reach back into my past to write this book, it amazes me how much I have blocked out, or lost, along the years of my life. My mind held onto certain salient details... and yet many years blend into the next without a proper story line or logical sequence of events. Perhaps it works well this way - forward, onward, the past is past and we hold onto whatever we need to support our dance presently, now, and that is all that really matters.

This book is a collection of reflections on bringing up children, while exploring a natural way of life and natural way of eating. I am not scientifically recommending one kind of diet over another objectively or ultimately, but simply exploring the innuendoes and joys of whole plant foods, which a growing number of families find themselves thriving on. Cooking and understanding natural whole foods using macrobiotic principles of energy and balance, is commensurate with a close to the ground, community way of life. For me, this approach makes sense on a small planet that is getting more crowded all the time; and opens up pathways to ever subtler sensitivity, flexibility, ease in body and clarity of mind.

My life partner Ted and I have had thirteen children together since 1980. In all those years of pregnancies and babies, we used community around simple plant based foods as our base, to make it all work. Many of the kids are now strapping handsome adults, and it is clear that we didn't need animal foods, nor traditional schooling, to create these healthy bright people... But that we did need whole grains and fresh vegetables, as well as some freedom to think and live differently.

These are quickly moving times, some say perilous times, but I say fascinating and full of challenge and change. Deep in every person on earth is a glimpse of the infinite, of ordinary endless cycles and seasons of which we are a part... The natural forces that lie deep in our operating systems are humming along in peace and contentment, as ever; and, we are slowly becoming more aware: exploring, growing, and playing with our friends, just like kids.

I am very grateful to Michio and Aveline Kushi, for pointing the way and inspiring this journey; and also to my Ionia co-founders: Bill and Megan Johnson, Michael and Victoria Becherer, and my parents Barry and Cathy Creighton - for clearing a path and keeping good company. I send thanks to my cooking and health theory teachers for putting themselves out there so I could catch some of their wisdom: Bill Tara, Warren Kramer, Denny Waxman, Mayumi Nishimura, Verne Varona, Jessica Porter, Mike Zeeb, Sandor Katz, Michael Pollan. I am deeply appreciative of my partner and love Ted, for his clear sight and companionship; and so grateful to the many children, for their bright energy and many laughs. Alaska has been a good home for us with its cold, clear air, dramatically changing seasons, endless wilderness and down-home, tolerant people - so I am thankful to Alaska itself, for allowing our dream to flourish here in the muskeg and spruce forest.

chapter one

BEGINNINGS

INTRODUCING MYSELF

"Don't ask what the world needs. Ask what makes you come alive and go do it. Because what the world needs is people who have come alive."
~ *Howard Thurman, theologian and activist*

My first memories of eating grains and vegetables are happy ones: I remember when I was perhaps seven or eight, sharing a bowl of hot mom-made barley mushroom soup with my grandpa at the kitchen table, savoring the creamy broth, my feet dangling off the chair, smiling back at his warm laughter. I also recall a summer afternoon on the porch stairs, when I was seven years old, dipping whole juicy boiled radishes into a small bowl of salad dressing, popping them into my mouth and biting off the stringy greens, the juice running in rivulets down my chin. For one of my young birthdays, I remember sinking little pink birthday candles into a watermelon.

At age six, my mother followed the man she loved to Boston, to study macrobiotics - a biological approach to world peace. It was 1970, and Michio and Aveline Kushi, both from Japan, were teaching a philosophy based in the order of the universe, yin and yang as dynamic forces of life and the wisdom of eating a plant based diet. Michio and Aveline were dynamic visionaries who shared a mission to teach about the power of food in ones' life. The Kushis both came of age in the second world war and following in the footsteps of George Ohsawa, Christoph Hufeland and others, they shared a dream of One Peaceful World. They moved to Boston with their five children, and started informal teaching, healing and counseling. They wrote books and began magazines, opened natural foods distributors, importers, stores and restaurants. In those heady days of change, anything felt possible, and in macrobiotic "study houses" all around metropolitan Boston there were over 4,000 young people and families involved.

For a good description of macrobiotics, I like my friend Verne Varona's definition: *"Macrobiotics is a compound word adapted from Greek, from the words, large (macro) and life (bios). As a dynamic philosophy of living, it defines itself as being a comprehensive way of life, offering invigorating principles that guide and educate, along with practical tools to strengthen body, mind and spirit. Recognizing that we are composed of many bodies: physical, intellectual, emotional, creative and spiritual, the macrobiotic way of life offers varied kinds of nourishment to sustain our collective growth. The ultimate goal of the macrobiotic philosophy is to create freedom; from fear, from sickness and from living lives of indifference. To be 'macrobiotic' is to have a personal goal of living and sustaining a large life."*

My mother said that to her, the Kushi's message was both far reaching and full of immediate common sense. After tasting her first bowl of savory sea vegetable soup and sweet brown rice at a friend's house in Boston, she knew that she must find out what this food was all about. It meant something significant to her, bigger even than physical nourishment. The meal relaxed her soul, it fed a budding consciousness she was barely aware of.

When I was seven, we moved into the new macrobiotic study house in Wakefield Massachusetts. I remember it as a huge old New England style manor house with rambling grounds and a rustic barn for me to run and play in. My mother and I shared a tiny clean room on the third floor. The great country house had hardwood floors and sparse, natural furnishings; we ate our meals with the thirty or so students family style, sitting on colorful zabuton pillows at long, low wooden tables. I remember the study house parents - senior Kushi students - being kindly towards me, gently teasing me about my struggles with the new foods. I enjoyed lingering in the kitchen with the housemother, watching her chop the unfamiliar vegetables in her brightly colored apron and handle her lovely wooden spoons.

My favorite foods at that time of my life were canned clam chowder, barbecued chicken and malted milk balls. The transition to brown rice with barley, hiziki (sea vegetable) with carrots and burdock and blanched kale was a bit surreal. Having a big group of kids and parents eating this way too - living together like summer camp - made it all more natural and easy. We kids would skip through the huge organic gardens, peering at the pumpkins to see if they were ripe, and then tromp like bulls through the dark dilapidated barn yelling loudly to keep our fears at bay. I remember the meals tasting more delicious to my young flexible sensibilities with each season.

As I grew up, whole foods and the ideas that were embedded in macrobiotics grew up within me and became an integral part of who I am. Macrobiotics meant interpreting humankind as an integral yet tiny part of an infinite universe. It meant paying more attention to the natural laws and cycles of the whole universe. My mother started a second family and as I daily helped cook meals for my brothers and sisters the principles involved in cooking and simple home self care became second nature. Several times as a young teen I listened to Aveline Kushi speak of her unrealized dream of creating a model agrarian village and it struck a deep resonant chord within me. I began to dream of raising a large family within a kibbutz-like community, a tiny town of our own making. I drew maps of a little village campus complete with community movie theater, gardens and laundromat. As far as I knew it didn't exist, but it lived and breathed in my daydreams... My favorite movies were Sound of Music (the true-ish story about a large family singing their way to solidarity in a Swiss alps village); the Emerald Forest (a tribal adventure amongst the indigenous rain forest peoples); and Fiddler on the Roof (the classic tale of generational change set in a rural nineteenth century Russian Jewish Shtetl) … I wanted to have a dozen children and raise them in our very own close to the ground village away from the absurdities of modern mankind.

As I grew older those absurdities began to have a crushing effect on my youthful spirit, bringing periods of despair and disillusionment. I felt fragile in the world. When I met my partner-to-be, Ted, who was struggling to survive as a carpenter in Boston, I thought that I recognized his unhappiness. He suffered hard symptoms of someone who didn't fit into modern aspirations, yet who had a hankering to live more intelligently, adventurously and naturally. Ted was traumatized by his affluent upbringing in ways that had potentially calamitous repercussions. Yet he also resonated the dream of "getting out of the amusement park and into the green hills of earth". We both needed natural whole foods and up-close support to find a livable state of mind. We both needed to do something about the things that made most sense to us.

My childhood village vision became our beacon. It pulled Ted and me together and it also propelled us to find others of like mind. Slowly, a small group of families with similar intent began to spiral around each other. In 1985, with our many children pushing us along, we were driven by desperation, hope, idealism and a touch of madness up to Alaska to find a secluded piece of land we could call our homeland. In the following Spring, these founding mothers and fathers purchased five acres of muskeg and spruce forest on the Kenai Peninsula in South-Central Alaska, and the village we came to call "Ionia" had its beginning.

INTRODUCING IONIA

"Shared sorrow is half sorrow. Shared joy is double joy." ~ *Nigerian proverb*

The four founding families of Ionia came from different geographic, cultural and socio-economic backgrounds, from California working class to East Coast blue blood, as well as different kinds of internal pressures. Most had behavioral illness diagnoses stemming from deep troubles with the culture around us.

In our chosen semi-isolation in the woods, through a process of trial and error, the families realized that each individual serves an essential role in a community, just as lungs and kidneys perform vital functions in a body. We also found that subjects are interconnected: that in order to sustainably change one thing, we had to change almost everything. To let go of the old and listen to the new, we had to find courage and curiosity, which only came from serious soul searching. To nurture our gathering, we found that we had to be able to stop struggling with, and pursuing, financial security… So we took steps towards voluntary simplicity, poverty, and pooling resources… And to be able to closely share resources, and raise our kids together, we had to forge out a flexible, shared vision and common language… which took sitting down to meet together daily. We had to have quieter nervous systems to tune into those meetings, to be adaptable and resilient in the details of our lives…. Thus, to quiet ourselves, we found it necessary to eat whole grains and vegetables. We each had different subjects which were most important to us, so we began to dance with each other, with our different cultures and strengths. And so, we found ourselves on a spiral of interconnected change.

Ionia is not a solution to problems, yet the founding process has set a precedent for walking into daunting challenges. We have found that that precedent, no matter how obscure or remote, can tip the scale toward positive change. The lush gardens and log beams, simple activity, grounded ideas and bright starlit Alaskan nights have a deeply rejuvenating and inspiring effect. We have come to see that it is impossible to create change in others, without embodying it ourselves – and that sustainable change moves in a spiral, rather than in a straight line. This kind of thinking has led to our endurance as a community, and eventually, as we relaxed, a force for positive change in Alaska.

Ionia's year round population now hovers around forty-five people, of all ages and abilities, from newborns to elders. In the warmer months, our numbers swell, as we take in new and old friends, dozens of residential volunteers, as well as give frequent day tours. We have become well known for our delicious macrobiotic cooking, pioneering spirit, peer support skills and explorations into varied natural building and growing methods. We are spoken of as "the Shire" or "our little commune"- usually with affection. We often partner with social service organizations, local food advocates, Native Alaskan tribes and state government to organize events and workshops that further our mission.

Ionia is all about the food. The second generation has begun to ferment foods in earnest: we now make mouth watering miso, shoyu (soy sauce) and ringo-boshi (salty/sour apples), wine, cider and sake, amasake (sweet rice ferment), tempeh (soybean cheese) and natto (sticky, stinky, fermented soybeans), sourdoughs, sauerkrauts, kimchees and pickles of all sorts. We regularly make fresh tofu, seitan (wheat-meat), mochi (sticky sweet rice pancakes), baby food and desserts from scratch. We pick wild sea vegetables, mushrooms, berries, greens and herbs, and dry some for winter eating. Our organic gardens grow thousands of pounds of bright, cool weather vegetables. We are experimenting with winter squashes, corn, beans, seeds and grains in our many greenhouses.

This bustling environment was born out of the dynamic combination of pressure and vision. We aren't sure if we are brave pioneers, idealists and visionaries, or if we are failures, mentally ill and unable to cope. Either way, we wouldn't or couldn't fit in to the busy structures of modern society. Some of the common sense views known as macrobiotics - or "large life" - gave us a practical pathway to channel our energies and dreams, pool our resources and strengths to create a post-post modern day village.... which has become Ionia. It's given the second generation a huge reserve of social capital. Our Ionia has become an authentic, natural way of life; an out of the ordinary environment to gather within, so that common sense can come alive. Our hope is that this way of life will continue to grow and deepen for many generations to follow.

LIFE AS WE KNOW IT

"The world breaks everyone; and afterward, some are strong at the broken places."
~ author Ernest Hemingway

Our mothers and fathers originally gave us our life... But the air we breathe, the environment, the world views we hold and the food we eat literally recreates and sustains our life every day. These forces stimulate our imagination in different directions, give us our stamina and determine who we are.

We all inherit a certain foundation, a spirit or nature - a mental, physical, emotional constitution - from our parents and ancestors. What we do with that inheritance after birth each day, each year, creates our condition. While one's constitution is set, ones condition is changing constantly, daily.

Somewhere along the way, once I quit school and had some time on my hands, I discovered for myself that daily food holds tremendous power to change my experience. I was a young teenager and would roam the Boston streets, curious and aimless. I decided to try a three day brown rice fast, chewing well, and was inspired and imprinted by the light emotional freedom that I felt. I experienced how my daily food feeds my direction. My bloodstream crucially and constantly feeds the chemical balance available to the brain - it can dull my senses, make me tired, push my emotions into high swings; it can also support clarity of mind and lightness of spirit, keep me calm and resilient.

Surely my condition is the lens through which I learn, and unlearn. It can contribute toward holding and storing emotion and excess deep in my body, or allow me to let it flow and go. My condition is created in my deepest intestines, aided by the microbes living and communicating there, and changes quickly - daily. By changing my bloodstream, I change my cumulative condition, my learning lens and my destiny.

FOOD AS ENERGY

"Without order nothing can exist - without chaos nothing can evolve."
~ unknown proverb

To understand cooking without recipes using macrobiotic traditions, one must begin by imagining the whole universe as one infinite stream of energy, vibrating, and pulsing, to create endless variety. Every thing in this world is made up of energy, and energy streams infinitely. This is not a mystical theory any more, through the explorations of modern day physics, it is a well explored fact. Living and dying, health and illness are two edges of the same wave. Ideas, emotions, light and sound waves, all physical things - even humans - are little spirals in this infinite stream of vibration... They appear like whirlpools in the ocean, become actualized as recognizable forms, then melt back into that infinite stream...re-form... and back again in an endless wave of creation and destruction.

Within the infinite ocean of energy, imagine opposite tendencies emerging: one of expanding, upward, outward, moister, slower, releasing, dispersing, yin. And one of contracting, downward, inward, dryer, faster, holding, gathering, yang. These opposite dynamics are complimentary, two manifestations of the same life force: the birthing and dying process, the push and pull of gravity and space, the atomic dance of neutrons and electrons, the magnetic poles of the earth, a heartbeat, breath, digestion and elimination, growth - these endless movements of existence manifest in predictable patterns of expansion and contraction, or "yin" and "yang". These movements define the world which we see and feel. As I get older, these patterns intuitively make more sense and I can see them as two sides of the whole in a pulsating, spiraling universe.

I also notice that as energetic creatures in this world, humans are taking in and releasing energy our whole life. We breathe in, we breathe out. We listen, we talk. We absorb, we create. We learn, we teach. We take in, we put out. We eat, we burn it up and discharge. And food is also, at its most basic, spirals of vibration or energy.... It is a whole bunch of atoms and particles, elements and chemicals, calories and nutrients, fuel for the fire of life. To play with food is to play with energy - how meals taste, feel, and what they create in us when eaten.

Raising children naturally, and on grains and vegetables, is an adventure! An infinite variety of possibilities is waiting to be explored. This book is my attempt to document some of that adventure.

This approach to life and energy, and specifically to food, is otherwise known as

MACROBIOTICS - OR - LARGE LIFE
(or the big picture).

chapter two

INGREDIENTS

THE BROADER PICTURE

"If you don't know where you are going, any road will get you there."
~ Lewis Carroll, author of Alice's Adventures in Wonderland

I like to tell my children that they can eat anything, as long as it is human food. Since many of the substances ingested nowadays are not actually food, this is a reliable tenet. It may also be worth thinking upon whether dairy - the perfect natural nourishment for baby cows or goats - is human food; or whether mammals and birds - the instinctive sustenance for carnivorous animals - are human food; or whether there is any "food" in white flour at all.

Another broad view on ingredients: foods that are whole nourish the trillions of micro-organisms that live within us and upon us. The genetic richness of our bacteria is infinitely more complex than our own, and serves as a buffer and interpreter of our environment. These invisible partners are integral to our balance and without their assistance we cannot thrive, or even live. Keep the microbes happy, and you will be joyful…. Conversely, unhappy microbes equals miserable person.

I find that if I stop to quiet down and listen to my body, it speaks to me, and only me. My system sends me signals, patiently and gently, about which foods it wants to eat. Therefore, ingredients are the language I use to speak back to myself, to keep that cherished confidential conversation going which lasts a lifetime.

Most everyone is familiar with the scientific nutrient based ways of determining the qualities within foods - calories, vitamins, minerals, fats etc. In this book, and in my life, I mostly set those distinctions aside and think more simply about foods in terms of:

- plant or animal?
- how concentrated is it?
- whole, partial or refined?
- and specifically, what kind of energy does it bring to the eater?

LET'S PLAY: IS IT ANIMAL, PLANT OR MINERAL?

"The belly rules the mind." *~Spanish Proverb*

Animals eat plants... Some animals eat animals who eat plants... Either way, the original source of all animals' energy is the plant kingdom. One could see animal flesh, eggs and milk products as more concentrated forms of plants, more energy dense. A steak has loads of calories packed into it compared to a bowl of brown rice and beans. The taste on the tongue is fatty and salty and the impact on the eater is more concentrated. Two acres of grass feeds one cow.... which can become 500 pounds of beef (or 500 hefty servings.) The same two acres planted in rice or millet becomes 12,000 pounds of grain (or 24,000 generous servings.) The same energy input is spread out over way more meals, making the energetic effects of grain based meals more diffuse.

Refined and processed sugars are also highly concentrated forms of plants. Common table sugar is exceedingly condensed from the original plant source, sugar cane or sugar beets. High fructose corn syrup is even more concentrated and refined - imagine an entire field of corn in every can of soda. The taste on the tongue is overwhelmingly sweet, immediately and it enters the bloodstream quickly right there in the mouth. The energy of refined sugars is that of a powerful and addictive stimulant, similar to cocaine. Even white rice, white bread, white pasta have very refined simple sugars and a fast burning addictive effect on ones appetite and energy levels.

Of course minerals are also highly concentrated, being in essence rocks, which take millions of years to form. They are hard and dense compared to plants. Everyone intuitively respects the concentration of minerals. If someone ate the same portion of salt as, say, bread, they would very quickly die!

I experience these animal foods and refined foods as concentrated and strong, and therefore to be treated with a lot of respect. Concentrated foods are very high octane fuels which create strong winds and high waves, prone to explosions, in the liquids of our body. Everyone, and every culture, intuitively strikes some kind of balance in order to sustain life. When eating strongly contractive and strongly expansive foods (meats and alcohol, for example) the balance looks more like a stormy sea, with high highs and low lows:

Energy levels, emotions and perceptions will have an equal swing, through mountains and valleys.

I experience whole plant foods as comparatively milder fuel, creating slower currents and calmer seas within. They have complex whole sugars and a multitude of essential nutrients which are processed more slowly in ones digestive system before they enter the bloodstream, with a gentler more sensitive effect. We can all experience that their immediate taste is more subtle (such as the sweetness in carrots). With whole plant foods (grains, beans, vegetables) the balance looks more like a smoothly flowing river:

Energy levels, emotions and perceptions become more level, spread out, gentle and steady. Nothing hits quite as hard nor boosts quite as much.

The balance within individual bloodstreams becomes the lens through which we experience events and circumstances... How quickly emotions are triggered, how hot they burn, how much focus can be summoned, how much stamina or flexibility is found; and therefore how we respond to the flurry of small and large challenges and potential stressors life has in store for us - these things are largely influenced by the quality of fuel in our bloodstream. That constant drip that is feeding our brain, and other organs, changes day to day depending largely on what we are eating, meal to meal. Over time, our condition changes and so does our experience.

Food is biological: whole foods crave whole foods, while concentrated, refined foods crave more concentrated, refined foods... Eating brown rice and millet creates a taste for lentils and kale. They need, crave and complement each other - they call for their friends. Eating hamburgers and french fries creates a taste for milkshakes and soda. They complement each other, crave each other and call for their friends, as well. A vortex emerges in which what we eat each day wants company - more of the same - spiraling around creating our ultimate destiny. It's a complex mechanism of desire, dream, appetite and biology. And it all starts with an idea about what to eat today. Understanding all this, and working/playing with it, is known in some circles as the practice of macrobiotics.

THE CULTURAL CONTEXT
(WHY DO WE EAT WHAT WE EAT?)

"We sense that 'normal' isn't coming back, that we are being born into a new normal: a new kind of society, a new relationship to the earth, a new experience of being human."
~ Charles Eisenstein, activist and author

Another thought about eating animal foods: In many cultures, serving meat means prosperity, while serving bread means poverty. More nutrients is seen as better, healthier, safer. If one eats millet and beans, it can mean that one is poor and worse, at risk, whereas if one eats meat and milk it is a symbol that one is wealthy and safe. These cultural symbols often semi-consciously define people's feelings about food.

I imagine that eating animals supports a more competitive paradigm of survival of the fittest based on the most nutrients going to the few who get it first.... where rich is better than poor. This has been the status quo for thousands of years. However, as it turns out, in these modern times with so many, many humans, there is not enough money nor meat to go around and trying to produce enough for this mindset is rapidly appearing to be planetarily unsustainable. I imagine that the modern dilemmas of this age old paradigm are going to absurdity. For example, America remains the symbol of a "chicken in every pot", bigger cars and bigger houses, the land of opportunity and prosperity.... However, most of the dis-eases running rampant over America today spring from the conditions of over-abundance and over-stimulation. America's dream of cheap, bountiful food has become a culture of corporate food and stealthy stimulants, which in the environment of the marketplace has become a glut of concentrated and addictive ingredients on a scale never before seen. The cheapest foods are heavily refined and processed: corn syrup provides plentiful and inexpensive calories in most of the grocery store brands. Anti-biotic medications and growth-boosting hormones in the plentiful burgers; GMO grown flours, powerful preservatives and powdered caffeine in breakfast cereals and drinks; vegetables with chemical colorings to make up for their lack of vitamins and minerals fill out the picture of food corporations run amok. The body easily becomes hooked to that fast rush of energy from simple sugars; the taste buds become desensitized to all but the strongest tastes, and the mind obsesses on quick easy eats wrapped in pretty packaging. So much concentrated concoction is proving too much for the human mind and body to comfortably handle. These sorts of paradoxes bring up writing new cultural stories, rewiring values and appetites, changing diets and changing minds.

Feeding ourselves plants, which are more diffuse and abundant, may support a more cooperative paradigm, one based on bounty for all, wherein less is actually more, and eating until one is 80% full, becomes sensual rather than punishing. Eating locally grown plants is a humble activity which supports a tolerant, seasonally aware way of life. To know the local food growers and producers; to seek out homemade ingredients; to renew and discover the secrets of making bread, jam and pickles or to forage wild foods - these simple activities lead to being more connected to nearby life forms, including neighbors.

Fostering alliances with microbes, in our bodies and in our soil, leads to a game changing awareness of the powerful, invisible world around and within us. Somewhere between free will and determinism, in the nooks and crannies between separation and oneness, our comprehension of human-ness evolves into an understanding that there is more than one species driving this bus. An acre of grain feeds many people, eating less. In my experience, less space, shared space, less dense activities and macro view of human society's place in the universe goes well with a plant based diet. I imagine the beginning of this new paradigm as young, but daily growing.

BASICS OF VARIETY AND BALANCE

"Eat food. Not too much. Mostly plants." ~ *Michael Pollan, author and speaker*

Because whole food has become kind of mysterious in these modern times when corporate packaged foods are all pervasive, this chapter details the ingredients to be found in a macrobiotic pantry. There are a huge diversity of grains, beans, land and sea vegetables, seeds, nuts, fruits and cooking seasonings which are key to supporting good cooking and whole health. Using variety to find balance is key to successful cooking without recipes. I include a whimsical sentence within each ingredient description imagining what would happen if I ate only this? What kind of condition would that create? This helps illustrate that variety is key: every front has a back, and a wide array of whole foods are needed for balance. Wonderful qualities when taken in excess become detrimental. (Strong in excess becomes stubborn, lightness overdone becomes weakness, centered becomes narrow, etc.)

Every kind of ingredient has qualities which it brings to the table (literally):

WHOLE GRAIN when well chewed and therefore not overeaten, is a miraculous clean burning fuel. It cleans out your system as it burns, leaving you refreshed and clear headed. It creates a gentle inner strength, like a plant stalk - sinewy and tough, yet flexible as well. Grains support a sensitive intelligence and conscious intuition. Whole grains have been the centering staple in human cultures forever, the "staff of life". It is the glue which holds together a complete, sustainable, whole foods diet.

Whole grain is very centering, grounding and deeply satisfying. It kind of leaves you alone. By eating the grain whole, you allow your body to find health. Children who are not sugared up always love whole grain. Well chewed brown rice is one of the strongest foods one can eat, it's truly kind of miraculous. I have lots of amazing stories about it. I experience that a meal without grain isn't really a meal at all - more like a snack. It is not quite as satisfying, and is hard to know when to stop. I have found that if well chewed whole grain is missing too long in my daily fare, I will start to feel deficient, and in the long term, depleted.

For practical purposes in the kitchen, think of these whole grains:

- the brown rices (including short, medium and long grain, sweet rice, basmati)
- millet
- whole oats (groats)
- barley (both hulled and hulless)
- quinoa
- corn (blue and yellow)
- the wheats - red, white, winter, spring (also Kamut, spelt and rye)
- buckwheat (kasha)

There are also some esoteric grains like jobs tears (hato mugi barley), amaranth and teff for adventurous souls.

Secondarily, there are the many whole grain products in which most of the whole grain is present, but has been ground up:

- whole grain pastas, and quality oriental noodles like soba and udon
- polenta and cornmeal
- corn tortillas
- whole wheat breads including pita and chapatis
- cracked oats, rolled oats (not instant)
- seitan ("wheat meat")
- bulgur
- whole wheat couscous

The advantages of eating whole grain products such as polenta or whole wheat noodles is that they are lighter and softer than their whole grain parents, easier to eat up front, faster to cook, add fun and lighter fare to weekly menus.

However, when considering grain, the rule is simple: the more processed a grain is, the less energy is held within. A bowl of brown rice, when well chewed, has three times as much energy to give us than an equal bowl of brown rice cream cereal (even though it has the same quantity of nutrients). If we refine it further by taking away the bran, making a bowl of white rice, then the grain loses even more energy. In fact, it will start to be an energy drain because, once consumed, our body has to work hard to "make it whole again" by trying to replace those lost vitamins and minerals.

There is a continuum available in modern times from... the WHOLE grain (such as whole wheat berries) to... cracked or milled (whole wheat flour) to... polished/ refined (bleached white flour) to... refined and processed with preservatives and sugars added (most white bread). These last two categories take more energy than they give, so they beg for more concentrated ingredients added in, such as butter or sugar. Keeping WHOLE grains in ones' meals ensures the integrity of your energy source.

What would happen if I ate only whole grain (and that's all)?
Grain has a very centering effect. Grain fasts for ten or even thirty days are cleansing, strengthening and amazingly healing. Well chewed grain gives one a will of iron. However, if I only ate grain, forever, I might become too sensitive and contracted for the ways of the world, inflexible, pure and one sided in my views and deficient in essential vitamins and minerals.

LAND AND SEA VEGETABLES
add a necessary array of nutrients and minerals to ones resources. Roots, round and leafy vegetables and delicious sea vegetables provide inner strength, outer glow and ease of movement for our whole body.

My experience is that children like vegetables best cooked fresh - still steaming, preferably. Many toddlers who usually turn up their nose at steamed broccoli will eat it a huge plate of it if they are sitting on the kitchen counter, with mom, eating it freshly cooked out of the pot. Sauces and dressings can help as well. With some experimenting, it is easy to find favorite vegetable dishes which will stand up over the test of several generations of children (sautéed kale with scrambled tofu is a tried and true big hit.)

ROOT VEGGIES (carrots, burdock, parsnip, daikon, turnips, rutabagas, radishes, celeriac, yams) are the strongest part of the plant (growing downward, rooted in the earth). They are warming, strengthening, add sweetness and hardiness to meals. They dig deep in the dirt, and give one the ability to dig deep into opportunities and situations. They especially nourish intestines and kidneys.

> *What if I ate ONLY root veggies? I might become tunnel visioned, recalcitrant and easily bothered by people and circumstances that get in my way. My inner organs might become too heavy, tight and malnourished.*

ROUND VEGGIES (cabbage, cauliflower, onions, squashes, kohlrabi, brussel sprouts) are very calming and nourishing. As vegetables go, they are centered between lightening and strengthening. They add sweetness and comfort to many dishes, and to ones' disposition. They lay on the ground and make us grounded, with a steady, calm foundation. They are especially beneficial for our stomach, spleen and pancreas and for regulating blood sugar.

> *What if I ate ONLY round veggies? I might become too bland and sedentary, with no get up and go.*

STEM AND LEAFY VEGGIES (kale, collards, mustards, napa cabbage, the greens of turnips and radishes, all the oriental choys, watercress, parsley, celery, scallions, broccoli) are the lightest part of the plant, growing upward and spreading out. They keep one flexible, fresh, and seeing outward. Greens keep us moving, light, fast and loose. They reach for the sun and keep us uplifted and joyful. They are full of vitamins and especially good for quick energy. We need and crave greens almost every day.

> What if I ate ONLY leafy greens? Perhaps I'd become very thin and hungry, forgetful, a victim, quickly blown over in the strong winds of life. My inner organs would become looser and weaker and my immune systems compromised.

SEA VEGETABLES (hiziki, arame, wakame, kombu - kelp - dulse, agar-agar, sea palm, nori) hold wonderful, essential minerals and are both quite flexible and quite strong. Seaweed flows in the wild waves, yet holds onto its little bit of rock, tenaciously. For us at Ionia who are mostly vegan, it is vital for our bones, teeth and hair, essential for pregnant and nursing moms, young children, elders and - well - everybody. A little bit of sea vegetable goes a long way to keeping our blood balanced, clear, and eyes bright. It gives one the quality of a mermaid - sparkling, adventurous and playful.

> *What if I ate only sea vegetables? Oh my - I might become like glass: easily shattered. I would be processing way too much salt and minerals, and contrarily would probably become deficient in minerals as my body worked overtime to wash them away.*

THE NIGHTSHADE FAMILY VEGETABLES and other acidic vegetables (tomatoes, potatoes, eggplants, tobacco, peppers, chard, spinach) are usually eaten as a good balance for animal-food eating cultures, but as one eats less animal foods, they become less appealing for several reasons. Nightshades are extremely acidic, inflammatory, sometimes even poisonous in their effect. Because of their high nicotine content, they are addictive as well. I eat them occasionally, almost as medicine. They have a loosening quality, which is sometimes valuable. As fun foods which are deeply embedded in our culture, it can be relaxing to cook with tomatoes or potatoes or peppers to make familiar dishes at holiday times or family reunions. However, as daily fare they are depleting in the long run.

> What if I ate only nightshades? I would crave red meat like crazy, and would experience weakness in my core - sexual organs, nervous system, heart - and inflammation in my joints and digestive organs.

MUSHROOMS and other fungi spread over the forest floor in the dark shade of big trees, moist, cool and hidden. They are very expansive and cooling to our systems as well. Dried mushrooms are more balanced and cooked into broths can loosen pockets of stuck energy, or fats, in our deep organs. Wild mushrooms grow everywhere, and when foraged with care, provide a gourmet pathway into locally sourced wild foods.

> *What if I ate only mushrooms and fungi? I would grow web-toes and mucous membranes instead of brains... Just kidding. However I would become quite weak, undernourished and easily cold.*

BEANS AND SEEDS add richness and fat (oil) to meals. They are relaxing, warming and deeply nourishing. Need I say more? They feed our inner organs and give a wide variety of vital nutrients, including protein. Beans and seeds are easily overeaten.

Children also love beans and seeds, and they especially need the rich fattiness. I often cook toddlers bean soups with diced vegetables and alphabet, or baby shell, noodles. My kids often cook themselves fried pinto beans or black beans as a snack, with tortillas or rice. My son Alex used to fry up chickpeas with onions, roll it in lettuce with mustard, and call it a bean roll.

Tofu and tempeh, Asian products made with the ultra-rich soybean, are also very popular forms of beans. Tofu is fabulous for sauces, sautés, tempura, stews, sandwiches, soup, you name it. It is relatively cooling. In contrast, tempeh is more warming, and great as a rich side dish or sandwich filling. Tempeh is easy to ferment at home and oh-so-delicious.

Here are the common beans and seeds:

- pintos
- kidneys
- soybeans
- chickpeas (or garbanzos)
- lentils
- navy beans
- lima beans
- black beans
- sunflower seeds
- sesame seeds
- pumpkin seeds
- chestnuts
- flax seeds

> *What if I only ate beans and seeds? WELL..... Perhaps I would become spoiled, satiated, unsatisfied and unhappy. Also, I'd have bad skin and bad digestion!*

OILS are necessary for most of us, add richness and essential fats and everyone finds them very delicious. As a result, they are easy to overdo. Who doesn't love deep fried foods? We use oil as a lubricant in our system, allowing energy and nutrients to move around and assimilate into our bones and organs... Yet when overeaten it has the opposite effect, hardening in our organs and sticking up the gears! Too much oil is the source of many salt and sweet addictions and is famously bad for our skin. Fried up leftovers are fabulous, but because most of us chronically overeat oils, it usually feels great to eat oil-less for a few weeks or even months every year. Additionally, in every meal I serve, there are at least some dishes without added oil. Cold-pressed unrefined vegetable oils are the cleanest burning in our system and digest best. Light and dark sesame, sunflower, and olive are my preferred every day oils.

We have been trying to grow sunflower seeds in the greenhouses, but so far only have grown sunflowers. If we were able to harvest the seeds, we could try to press oil like I once saw olives being pressed (in a huge, heavy, fly wheel press). Most of our oils are grown in quite tropical weather, so, someday, we would love to upgrade to a locally grown source.

> *What if I only ate only oils? My body would soon violently reject my choices.*

SALT, which is a mineral, is the most contracted, condensed substance anyone will ever eat. It's vital that everyone eat it. Therefore, good quality sea salt which is unrefined and has trace minerals (and no additives) is very important for health. Any damp salt (indicating that it is sun dried) will do. Playing around with the correct amount of salt for you is vital, and when found, is a very good source of energy. In macrobiotic cooking, salt generally is cooked into food, rather than added at the table. This helps quiet salt cravings. Getting amounts of salt right for long lasting health is a life long discovery - but I can say this: If and when one stops eating store bought processed food (bread, crackers, chips, cereal, candy, donuts, canned foods or boxed mixes) and/or animal food (primarily meat, eggs, and cheeses), then one will have also stopped a huge intake of salt that comes along with all that. So, if one is no longer eating a lot of those foods, one may need more salt in ones' home cooking.

> *What if I ate only salt? I would die very quickly and uncomfortably.*

On the other hand, salt, like sugar, is very addictive and easily manipulates our taste buds. Taste buds are sensitive and malleable, they adapt to concentrated amounts of salt and sweet very quickly. Thus, amounts of salt and sugar are very subjective, depending on a person's recent history with salt and sugar. After a few months of not eating white sugar, it burns the tongue. From the opposite end of the spectrum, after eating a few candy bars, a carrot tastes like dirt. It's the same with salt. Knowing this, one can easily manipulate ones' taste buds to cook, eat, and enjoy the amount of salt that one feels good about, over time.

> A MOM'S WARNING: Children are small and quickly growing... so they need way less salt than adults. I feed babies minuscule amounts of miso, and sea vegetables, added to their foods with no other added salts. If babies and little children do eat too much salty, dry food, (which is very contracting and tightening) they can become irritable, unreasonably stubborn and fitful; grinding teeth, leg cramps, and charlie horses can also emerge. A hot bath helps to remedy this overly tight condition. For young toddlers, too much salty cooking can even inhibit the absorption of nutrients and, over the long haul, create stunted growth and/or deformed bones. I had a child suffer from this, so I am quite mindful of salt now.

F**RUITS,** with their simple sugars and acidic nature, are quite expansive. While still whole, and not nearly as concentrated as highly processed foods, fruits are still more concentrated than carrots or barley, because of their high sugar and oil content. They are fun, quickly enjoyed and add fast bouncy energy to the day.

Children love raw fruit, but too much can weaken their immune systems, make them cranky or touchy, crying and wailing a lot and prone to drooling (for babies), stuttering (toddlers), runny noses, and infections if they eat too much. The acidity of fruit sugars also easily leads to a diaper rash. Cooked fruit desserts are less acidic, satisfy the common craving for sweets, while being soothing and relaxing.

N**UTS,** lightly roasted, with their abundance of oils, add crunch and make one jolly, if not overdone. A little bit goes a long way, however.

It is more strengthening of ones' immunity to eat fruits and nuts grown in similar climate to your own. For temperate climates: berries, apples, pears, cherries, peaches, plums, nectarines, olives, persimmons and kiwis, almonds, chestnuts, pecans, hazelnuts and walnuts are best. Leaving the bananas, avocados, oranges, figs, coconuts, pineapples, mangos, and cashews, peanuts, macadamias, pistachios to our more tropical cousins for regular eating will give one more vitality to work with, in the long run. Living in Alaska, my favorite fruits are wild strawberries, with blueberries coming in a close second. Wild berries are full of good stuff, and you can taste it. The sweetness of these delectable little treats isn't as acidic I find, if eaten in the sun, while watching billowy clouds form over the spruce tops.

> *What if I ate only fruits and nuts? I would probably become very weak, whiney or crying, confused, easily irritated, and easily cold. I would be accident prone. Over time, my intestines and brain would loosen and weaken, and consequently my immune system and nervous system would be compromised.*

O**THER** V**ITAL** C**OOKING** S**EASONINGS**
In a well balanced, whole foods diet these cooking seasonings are indispensable:

M**ISO** is a salty, earthy creme used for hearty flavoring of soups, stews, porridges and pickles. Miso is made from soybeans and barley or rice koji (which is the starter, or inoculant) fermented with salt for at least one year. Miso has beneficial organisms creating enzymes which are vital for digesting whole grains. (In meat eating cultures, yogurt and cheeses were used for this same purpose.) In grain eating households, miso and shoyu are key to feeding the microbes which assimilate all the valuable nutrients in the food. My family eats miso soup every day. Also Ionia now makes miso, from scratch. Like wine, each locale has its own bacteria and environment, creating subtle, distinct flavors.

SHOYU is known by many westerners as soy sauce. A fermented salty, rich, soybean/wheat seasoning used in just about everything: soups, stews and broths, porridges, sautéing, dressings, sauces and pickles. Shoyu flavors a broth similar to bouillon, is a gentler, more rounded form of saltiness and also holds those beneficial enzymes. I use shoyu in just about every meal. It adds that elusive, yet sought-after, deep flavor known as umami.

UMEBOSHI PICKLED PLUMS and ume vinegar are made from green plums, pickled in salt and shiso leaves (also called beafsteak leaves - a tasty herb) for a year or more. Umeboshi brings a unique, appetizing, bold combination of sweet/salty/sour to many dishes. It is bright pink and also bravely stands out as a healing power. Umeboshi is used as a go-to tonic for nausea, indigestion, and hangovers... also as a way to countermeasure poisoning of any mild sort. It is a strong, immediate counter-measure to an overly acidic condition. I use it often in dressings, sautés, pickles, and it is a great pickle on its own with brown rice. The juice off of the pickling crock is bottled and sold as ume vinegar. (I am beginning to make umeboshi from scratch, using Alaska's abundant sour crab apples instead of plums.)

KUZU (also spelled kudzu), processed from a root, is a thickener similar to corn starch which is very strengthening for the intestines. Perfect for adding to cooked fruits as it nicely balances the acid in most fruits and makes a satisfying dessert. It can also make a delicious clear gravy for sautéed veggie stir-fry. Kuzu is expensive, so I use it sparingly and consider it precious.

BROWN RICE VINEGARS are top of the list for adding zing and sour sparkle to dressings and pressed salads. Brown rice mirin is a jaunty sweet wine used to bring a touch of sweet to broths and sautés.

BROWN RICE SYRUPS are gentler than maple syrup, agave or honey. Brown rice syrup has complex sugars (rather than simple sugars) which are even gentler than fruit sugars and less acidic. As a sweetener, this is as mild as it gets and kids don't bounce off the walls after eating brown rice syrup. I use rice syrup in dressings, tea and desserts - pies, cookies, cremes and fruit compote. The kids simmer rice syrup down to make chewy crackly candies like taffy, peanut brittle and sticky popcorn balls.

HERBS AND SPICES are often used too indiscriminately and will drown out simple whole foods cooking, but a taste of ginger or garlic, a hint of basil or mint, some cilantro or dill are all welcome additions to the palette and add some nice balance or kick to meals. Soups and fried foods especially benefit from a bit of herbs as a garnish.

KUKICHA TEA is the twigs from the tea bush, which have no caffeine and make a very non-stimulating and non-intrusive drink. Kukicha makes a wonderful hot tea with desserts or to complete the meal. Simply simmer for five minutes and steep.

CONTINUUM OF ENERGIES:

Nothing being purely expansive or purely contractive, all foods (just like all things) manifest on a continuum.

EXPANSIVE ▼ YIN

MOST DRUGS & CHEMICALS
MARIJUANA
CORN SYRUP & SUGAR
CAFFEINE
SOFT DAIRY
HONEY
TROPICAL FRUITS, SPICES AND NUTS
TEMPERATE FRUITS AND NUTS
LEAFY VEGETABLES AND MUSHROOMS
ROUND VEGETABLES
ROOT VEGETABLES
SEA VEGETABLES
BEANS
SEEDS
BIGGER GRAINS
SMALLER GRAINS
WHITE MEAT FISH
RED MEAT FISH
HARD DAIRY
BURNT FOODS SUCH AS COFFEE
EGGS
WHITE MEAT
RED MEAT
SALT

CONTRACTIVE ▲ YANG

chapter three

FAMILY

FROM WOMB TO WEANING

In a dark moment I ask, "How can anyone bring a child into this world?" And the answer rings clear, "Because there is no other world, and because the child has no other way into it."
~ Robert Brault, American writer

When I was a girl, I always wanted a big family with a dozen children. When I was fifteen years of age, I was already searching seriously for a life partner. I needed someone who would resonate my dream of beginning a macrobiotic small scale "Shtetl" (village), and someone who would support my desire for a large family. I was the oldest, most serious teenager I knew. When I met Ted, I knew he was a very good candidate for such an adventure…. He was resourceful, insightful, he was broken down by society's expectations that he would never meet which made him desperate, and I saw that he had the emotional capacity to dig deep.

In 1980, when I became pregnant for the first time at age seventeen, despite the flush and drama of a new marriage, my diet was on my mind. All of a sudden what I ate was partly determining the fate of a whole other person. In those early weeks of the embryo's development, growth is happening at an unimaginable pace - each cell multiplying to become the bedrock of a person's constitution, a foundation for the rest of their life. My baby's future limitations and possibilities stared back at me from the bottom of my bag of french fries and my feelings about this were overpowering.

This pressure changed me. Gone was the freedom and fresh foolishness of youth. Gone were the days of binge chocolating and weekend pizza. In my new found role of mother, I lost some of my teenage angst and discovered a meaningful channel for all that young energy: cooking for my new family.

I cooked and ate ALOT, with gusto; I ate for two with plenty of confidence and much of my day was taken up with food. I wouldn't eat processed food or snacks but I had to compromise about organics because we had no money at all. We were completely broke, living in a questionable neighborhood of San Francisco. I took my food stamps to the cheapest oriental grocery store each day to purchase a few roots and that days' fresh new relative of choy (bok-choy, ming-choy, joy-choy). I was beside myself with delight when artichokes were on a dollar sale. I carefully weeded through the free offerings at the food bank for whole foods, without any sugar and additives: look - a bag of popcorn! pinto beans! raisins! Once, the Salvation Army gave me sixty pounds of whole wheat berries and I was so excited at the prospect of fresh flour. If only I could grind my wheat? All around town, I posted signs that read, "Seeking flour mill to grind sixty pounds of wheat, can pay a grinding fee. Please help out a young mom". One day, a kind eyed, neatly dressed, middle aged woman from the Seventh Day Adventist Church invited me to her home, to use her electric mill. So, on the bus I lugged my wheat. Her mill was powerful, and quite quickly, I was able to grind all of the wheat into lovely whole wheat flour for making bread.

My baby's clothes were hand sewn from cotton clothes found in the free box at the thrift shop, but he would be happy and healthy because I was cooking for us every day. I ate mochi (sticky rice pancakes)* with sesame seed sauce (made from toasted sesame seeds ground in my mortar and pestle) and blanched vegetable salad at every lunch for three months. I cooked chickpea soup and ate three bowls of it. I baked pies and cookies with mild sweeteners, and raced Ted to devour the entire dessert at one sitting. Eating good whole food was our glue, our way of keeping our feet on the ground, our hopes up and our eyes on the horizon.

When my son John Emrys came into this world all rosy and shining my pressures about cooking changed. Now, food became about milk production and infant rhythms; cooking happened between nursing and

see full explanation of mochi, page 35

Here is the bread I made then:

Rice Kayu Bread

1) Start with a good amount of leftover grain. Add water until you have a porridge consistency (you may need to soak it until the grains open up and become soft.)

2) Add a spoonful of miso and add whole wheat flour slowly until an elastic dough is formed. Knead and knead until it is the texture of your earlobe, adding flour as needed.

3) Divide the dough into two - four loaves. Shape the dough into loaves by turning, rolling and folding each into a cylinder.

4) Oil bread pans. Drop each loag gently into the pan, smooth side down, then flip it, so that it seam side down and all sides of the loaf are oiled. With a knife, cut a long slit along the top of the loaf. Place in a warm spot for six hours, to rise.

5) After six hours, steam the bread for two and a half hours. This is done by placing the loaf pans in a bath of water inside a large shallow pot. The water should reach the tops of the loaf pans, but no higher. You may need to replenish the water during the steam. Alternatively, a restaurant style rectangular steamer is ideal.

6) After more than two hours of steaming, the loaves will have risen to golden, fluffy, sweet cake-like bread. Cool, cut into slices, and serve with your favorite topping or spread.

---

changing diapers. I easily felt completely overwhelmed and helpless. Nursing babies eat everything their mother eats, yet they are little and have little defenses. Therefore the effects of our diets are more focused in infants. When I ate sugars, even fruit sugars, my baby got a diaper rash. When I ate too many salty chips, he became too contracted and would cry unusually and fitfully. When I got upset or uptight, my milk dried up. When John napped, I napped and when he smiled, I smiled back. How could I let that smile down? So I was caught - caught in the net of affection, a cycle of self care and self pity, trapped by my own idealism into cooking well and eating simply.

In the next few years my girls, Katie Eve and Jane, came along in rapid progression. Our unlikely journey toward small-scale community had led us back to Boston, the center of the macrobiotic movement. We were attempting to gather with a few other prospective families, including my mother Cathy, her husband Barry and their five youngsters. We were definitely on the bottom rung of the income ladder and we all rented a shabby duplex in a traditionally Irish neighborhood of Jamaica Plains. The arboretum and subways were nearby, so I often took the toddlers in our double stroller for walks and rides around the city for affordable amusement. In the collective house, we set up our basic kitchen (place where we cook nourishment for our bodies) and our "yin kitchen" (place where we cook vision and nourishment for our minds) and set up shop as a community trying to be born.

Chubby blonde Katie, age nine months, would sit in the middle of our living room rug watching the many people coming and going, a rock of calm in the midst of a churning river. She rarely cried. While I was nursing Katie, I followed my housemates into late night snacking sessions and ate countless toasted English muffins smothered in peanut butter and fruit jams, naturally made chocolate ice cream and apples with organic cheese. The late night conversations were much too fascinating to miss. It was the first time in a few years I had loosened the reins on my diet. Katie, my little Buddha baby, seemed to process my dietary transgressions by becoming very round and sedentary. (Later in her teenage life she developed difficulty with congestion, for which I always felt guilty. Dairy food, bread and nut butters, I am convinced, helped to cause this condition.) When Katie's sixteenth month came along and she was still not walking, I took her to see a pediatrician to check up on her development. The doctor, though he could identify no specific complaints, let me know sternly that, as far as he was concerned, I was under-nourishing my children by practicing a vegan diet, and that their development would suffer. It was not long afterwards that Social Services knocked at our door, spurred by the complaint that we were feeding our children seaweed. Come right in, yes we are! They soon closed our case, but these two incidents, for better or worse, pushed along a growing paranoid avoidance of medical professionals which lasted well into my parenthood. It was unfortunate, because Katie eventually walked just fine, and she grew like a weed.

My pregnancy with Jane, in fall of 1984, was one of the only times in which I had serious morning sickness – a miserable, misnamed state of being because nausea can last all day. Probably because of all that late night dairy eating in the previous six months, I paid my penance in that special hell that only pregnant women and cancer treatment patients experience. When I felt sick I couldn't eat brown rice of any kind, so I experimented with other grains and grain products. Eventually I had some luck with buckwheat, as well as corn tortillas. Soba noodles (made from buckwheat) cooked up, plain, with a few splashes of shoyu (soy sauce) and some scallions became my solace and my salvation.

I have seen other women in that state be able to tolerate buckwheat as well, especially cooked plain, without roasting, oil, or much salt. In those days, I didn't know how to cook dried corn as a grain, but I later discovered it to also be a useful staple for the weeks when morning sickness prevails. It turns out that whole, natural corn comes in many forms for human consumption: the most commonly known is tender sweet corn on the cob, steamed to perfection in hot days of late summer. But a denser, larger kerneled corn is also grown, dried and sold in bulk bags as a grain, mostly for preparing corn flour, masa and tortillas. To cook grain corn, one must soften it first with agricultural lime, or wood ashes from a wood stove.

I have had a lifelong love affair with corn - the happy food - both fresh as a vegetable, and dried as a grain. It is the quintessential American crop it seems to me. There are romantic images of Hopi Indians harvesting the red, yellow and blue kernels and filling up their baskets for the winters. I love corn chowders, stews, salads and corn masa (which is dough made from cooked grain corn.) Fresh corn cut off of it's cob is a luscious addition to almost any fresh vegetable dish, as well as soup. It adds a fresh summery energy.

Perhaps corn helped to shape Jane's character. When Jane was small, she had a little pixie face and giddy curiosity about life. Her favorite way to eat was to sit on my lap and laugh at all the goings on of the bigger kids, while I aimed each spoonful into her mouth. It is amazing to witness that small children's underlying nature never really changes as they grow up. Jane is still the same way, laughing and winking her way through her meals with friends.

I discovered early that I loved the feelings of pregnancy, of this little alien being springing up inside my body; the kicks

GRAIN CORN

4 cups of dent or flint corn
8 cups water
1 cup wood ash

1) Sift wood ash through a strainer to remove all the small chunks of charcoal.

2) Soak all the ingredients together overnight.

3) In the morning, bring up to pressure on high heat then simmer for 50 minutes on a low flame and heat diffusing pad ("flame tamer").

4) Remove from heat, let the pressure come down, empty the corn into a colander. Rinse all of the wood ash out. Mix and massage with your hands under running water until it is completely clean.

5) Place the washed corn back into a clean pressure cooker and add enough water to just cover the top of the corn in the pot.

6) Add a few pinches of salt, bring to pressure again on high heat and simmer on low with a pad for 40 final minutes.

Serve hot with pickles and beans. It is especially delicious fried up the next day.

Alternatively, for a rich porridge: after rinsing out the wood ash, add lots of sweet vegetables and simmer for 1 hour, adding miso for flavor at the end.

and burps and sore backs were part of the thrill of watching that belly grow. I leaned into the adventure of birth and liked to labor by myself. I devoted time to study and preparation, read all the birth books, gathered attention, caught the adrenalin and serotonin rush, rallied for the pain and intense push and reveled in the euphoria, almost like an athlete. It was part of mothering, connecting me somehow to the earth and the simple forces of nature.

After each baby came, I crawled into bed with this tiny creature and rested for one full month. I feel strongly that this is necessary for complete rejuvenation, for regaining ones' long term strength. I slept and nursed, mesmerized and exhausted. I stared at the baby for hours while quietly dealing with healing. I let myself get to know this new relationship, which would be around for many years ahead, and re-find center after the last nine months of pregnancy. I have come to highly value this four to five weeks of quiet time, for gaining back my endurance and fit body after the shock of birth. I let others in my life cook and clean. In the early years this person was Ted – my main support – who cooked me strong, vibrant food during this vital time in our life together.

My personal favorite dishes after birth include hiziki seaweed sautéed with lotus root, carrots and burdock root; wakame (another sea vegetable) cucumber salad; bean stews of all kinds but most especially aduki beans with winter squash; and soba (buckwheat) noodles in broth. More strengthening foods good for after birth include nishime*, kinpira*, and other well cooked root vegetable dishes; short grain brown rice chewed well; pressed salad *; and most especially fried mochi patties in miso soup.

We have found this dish to be guaranteed to give a mother tons of rich breast milk within hours. I always ate it once or twice each day in the first two weeks after birth - then as desired thereafter, for the many months of breastfeeding. It is melt in your mouth scrumptious!

for details on how to prepare pressed salad, kinpira and nishime, see pages 69, 71, and 75.

Magic Mochi Patties in Miso Soup
Make as much or as little mochi at a time as you like. It will keep in the fridge for up to a week.

A) Basic Mochi Dough:
equal parts sweet brown rice and water
a few pinches of sea salt

1) Combine ingredients in a pressure cooker and soak for 6 - 10 hours.

2) Bring to pressure on a high flame, then place a "flame tamer" (heat diffuser pad) under your pot and simmer on low for 20 minutes. Remove from heat and let it come down from pressure.

3) While still hot, pound vigorously with the biggest wooden pestle you can find, a clean wooden baseball bat or potato masher, for 15 minutes, until the rice starts to resemble a sticky dough.
~ OR ~ alternatively, push the rice through a Corona hand flour mill (using a pestle to press the rice through the mill) to produce a sticky dough.

4) Flatten the mochi dough into a tray or lasagna pan with a spatula, or with your hands
(keep your spatula or hands wet for easiest handling).

5) Store in the fridge until you are ready to prepare it for eating.

NOTE: Mochi is very sticky. Handling your mochi dough is much easier if you dip your pestle and spoons into a bowl of water as you go. Each time after making mochi, the mill will need to be taken apart, soaked, and then washed thoroughly.

Commercially made mochi is one of the few ingredients which are similar in taste and quality to homemade. If you happen to be lucky enough to be near a store which carries mochi, and you can afford it, go ahead and use the store-bought version.

B) Fried Mochi Patties:

1) Heat up a pan with fair amount of sesame oil on medium heat. Spoon a chunk of mochi into the pan and let fry for ten minutes, until golden brown and crispy. It will start to melt into a pancake in the pan - help it along with your spatula.

2) Once it is crispy and golden on the bottom side, flip the mochi patty over and fry until golden on the opposite side. Add more oil as desired as you fry, turning the flame down if it starts to stick.

3) When crispy and golden on each side, place on a platter. Top with raw sliced scallions.

C) Miso Soup:

onion, sliced in thin half moons
other sweet vegetables, sliced thinly
handful of wakame sea vegetable, soaked in water to rejuvenate
water to fill the pot
barley or brown rice miso to taste

1) Layer the onions in the bottom of a soup pot, and add water to cover. Bring up to a boil and simmer for 5-10 minutes. Add any sweet vegetables that you have - carrots, daikon radish, cabbage, squash, turnips, leeks - also sliced thinly. Layer the vegetables one at a time, hardest to softest, in the simmering water.

2) Add enough water to make a brothy soup and let it come to a gentle boil.

3) When the soaking wakame is soft and shiny, slice in small bite sized pieces. When the veggies are soft, add the wakame to the simmering broth. Cook for 5 minutes, then turn off the flame.

4) In a separate bowl, with a spoon, mix some miso with a bit of water. Blend up well until the miso is creamy and pourable. Add the mixture into your soup, to taste. The broth should taste mildly salty as well as sweet.

To serve: Pour a generous portion of miso soup over your fried mochi patty, in a bowl. Eat while hot! If you are breast feeding and need more, or richer, milk, eat this in the morning and again later in the day. Now wait for the milk to come…. Look out, the entire family will want to eat this every morning as well!

Mochi is very nourishing, warming, relaxing and fattening. (Toddlers love it because it is so rich and sticky and teenage boys love it for building up muscle mass.)

Much has been written about the lifelong benefits of feeding newborns naturally with mother's milk. It is indeed the perfect food for growing healthy humans. Colostrum, which is flowing in the first days after birth, gives baby an irreplaceable lifelong immune system boost. My latest favorite discovery is that there is complex communication that goes on between the microbial community living in and on mom's breasts and the microbes in baby's mouth – designed so that babies, by sucking on their mother's nipple, get on-going protection from pathogens and diseases in his direct environment. Apparently they are discovering that the microbes adapt, on the spot, according to what baby puts into his hands and mouth. How cool is that?

My babies were all very fat and healthy. Clearly, despite what some books may still say, a pregnant or nursing woman does not need animal food to thrive and produce big, healthy children. There are plenty of nutrients in grains, beans, seeds and the wide array of vegetables to feed a hungry growing pregnancy, and beyond. This is a culturally instilled worry we can leave behind, just as we abandoned the concern about falling off the edges of the earth. (Whew - one less thing!)

I was pregnant with my son Gregory Yukon, in 1986, when Ted and I, with three toddlers, drove up the endless Northern ALCAN highway. In a little blue Honda Civic, with our scant belongings, we drove from campground to campground from Dawson Creek in British Columbia, through the pretty town of Whitehorse in the Yukon Territories, across the Interior of Alaska and West to the coastal city of Anchorage. We rented a small cheap apartment on Jackass Lane for the winter. It was plain, with only a few furniture pieces, but we filled it up with yelling, giggling kids and good food aromas. In honor of the traditional Alaskan sourdough tradition, Ted baked lovely loaves every week of sesame and poppy seed breads, raisin walnut buns, rye toast. I ate it all up. My condition became quite tight and contracted from all this baked goodness, and one symptom of this was that I would often experience pressure on my back vertebrae, causing paralysis and pain. I started a daily yoga practice to help with my back, driving all the way downtown to the yoga center, which was a haven of tranquility. However, all that driving around probably pressurized me even more. It is a crazy paradox of city life: motor down the hectic crowded highway, in-between changing diapers and food shopping and feeding the family, to stretch and relax with other women.

I was attending such a class in February, when my contractions came on. By the time the class was over, I barely was able to hobble to the car, breathing heavily through the force of labor. Twenty long minutes later, I arrived home to our apartment and scared the children by roaring orders at Ted to set up a mirror, scissors, blankets, towels, phone. In moments, Gregory charged out like a bull. I handed him over to Ted and the other gawking children and then had the time to sit back, breathe, eat some warm stew with toast and reflect on my good fortune. Due largely I feel to my overly tight condition, this was by far my speediest birth and Gregory has been speeding about ever since, mentally quick and physically zippy.

In August, 1987, we moved from the city to our new land by the Kasilof beaches with the other founding families. For a $300 down payment, we had a beginning on ten acres of spruce trees and muskeg, the rolling mosses of the northlands. We purchased tipis, hired a local contractor with big bulldozers to clear a road and dig a well. Our tipi had sleeping rolls from end to end, as well as a wood burning cookstove, a thirty gallon tank of water heated by the wood fire and an old, but clean, bathtub. I often cooked fried wakame sea vegetables, fried black beans and hearty root vegetable stews on that cookstove, which could really crank out heat.

Winter came early with plenty of deep snow. The kids donned head to toe snowsuits and played out in the woods for most of each day. Gregory was one year old and his siblings bundled him up and dragged him around on a baby sled we made out of an old wooden crate. It was a fast ride, and he would return, as the pale sun sank below the spruce trees, with a chapped, red nose and cheeks. In the long evenings, we all huddled by the hearth, read, wrote letters, talked, played cards, made plans and sometimes bathed in our luxurious hot tub.

Once Spring break-up broke, we built. The women and children hand peeled every log. The stronger men lifted the logs into place (just like Lincoln logs) finishing one rough hewn 24 x 28 foot cabin at a time, before moving onto the next one. My older children began to cook that Summer. John was barely past toddler status, but, by necessity, he learned to cook a satisfactory pot of brown rice, beans and greens for the family. Three year old Katie helped as she could.

The Alaska Summer stretched out and blurred into one long, shining, golden day of vivid wildflowers, sweet berries and another round of logs to peel. It was phenomenal! The children's faces were stained purple with berry juices and swollen around the eyes with stinging bites from the black flies, who had been disturbed by our land clearing.

We built, and built, and built, one cabin shell, then another. We moved quickly to beat the encroaching autumn, which arrived suddenly with a series of frosty mornings and exited into bitter winter a few short weeks later. When the snow came, in early October, the final roof was not quite up, so that we were scraping ice chips off of the massive log purlins to lay down the pine tongue-and-groove roof boards.

When our basic cabin was up, the family took a day off of peeling logs to move into our new home. As I was settling the beds in place, I looked up to see that the children were creating a little sand castle in the middle of the soon to be living room with their shovels. They had become so accustomed to living outdoors, that they didn't make the distinction between outside and inside anymore! They figured that this was just one more treehouse to play in.

In the bone chilling January of 1989, we were cozied into our new log cabin. The roof was up, and there was an open floor plan with a loft. In one corner, Ted had built a lovely kitchen with a stainless sink, thick wood beam counters and pine shelving. Our faucets were plumbed with running cold water only, and we still had our trusty wood cookstove complete with a tiny baking oven. Another wood heater cranked in the corner, day and night, radiating heat into the cold log walls. We had thick wool rugs on the floors, where the babies played. Upstairs in the loft, each child had their own little corner which held a futon bed with a thick down comforter, and two hand-made wooden chests full of their clothes and belongings. Each child had their own interests, including the usual - sticker books, legos, markers and paints, collections of animals, photos and books - as well as stone collections, wildflower presses and clay from the beach. The kids liked to keep their "goodies" in little locked boxes, which they built out of scrap wood with metal hinges and hasps. (Although it wasn't long before they figured out that they could easily open each other's goody boxes with a screwdriver!) The kids mostly liked to play at my feet near the kitchen stove and we had long discussions while I cooked. It was dark much of the time. There was only tough, clear plastic sheeting, instead of glass, in our windows and doors. When the temperatures sank to thirty below zero, we were dismayed to see lines of frost penetrating into the corners of the house.

Ginger Fried Wakame

1) Soak a handful of wakame for 10 minutes or until it is open and tender.

2) Slice a small piece of fresh ginger into thin matchsticks (the more the better!)

3) Slice the wakame into bite-size pieces.

4) Generously coat a cast iron pan with sesame oil, heat to sizzling and add the ginger. Stir fry for several minutes over a hot flame until it begins to crisp up.

5) Squeeze dry the wakame, and add it into the pan. Stir quickly, adding a bit more oil if desired.

6) Sauté for five minutes until completely tender and season with shoyu to taste.

Garnish with sliced scallions and serve hot with brown rice or other grain.

Ted spent a good part of the short winter days out in the woods, locating dead standing spruce. He cut the tree down with a chainsaw, limbed it with an axe, and dragged or carried it to the wood lot where he sawed it into rounds. Now it was ready to be chopped into pieces that fit into the wood stoves. I enjoyed working with an axe, but was far slower than Ted, and I didn't have the upper arm strength to wield my way through a hefty knot. It was often the children's job to load the firewood into our big wheeled cart, or sleds, deliver it to the house and make big stacks under the eaves.

As my pregnancy progressed, my ease with an axe decreased. I was eight months pregnant with this baby # 5 when he decided to arrive early. I labored easily, familiar now with the pace and pain of my birthing process. When Alexander was born, on a clear frigid evening, he seemed somehow translucent, not quite finished. We bundled him under my thick comforter. Ted moved my bed directly in front of the wood heater, far away from the chilly corners and encroaching frost lines. He brought me steaming hot soups, and sweet vegetable rice porridge, every few hours and Alex and I lived under our personal bed tent for his first weeks of life, staying warm. When the weather finally broke, Alex was fattening up and yelling as lustily as he was nursing.

Four more sons - Lauden, Aaron, Connor Martin and James Galen - were born in our log cabin in rapid succession, with little fanfare, yet happy crowdedness. Those birth days are sweet memories full of the fierce overpowering warmth of a baby's arrival into the world. These boys formed the center of our family, the keel of the boat, keeping us afloat in stormy weather.

In-between meals, we talked, built, gardened, gathered firewood and talked some more, searching and losing and finding our shared vision for a common future. Here we were living together in the frozen north, imagining an alternate upside down, natural world, like hobbits. All of the founding families had many children. It was as if the children themselves were hurtling us toward our destiny. There was a force about this large family, this noisy nest of young energy, that led me down the community path with much exuberance and hope. There is an inherent optimism in the act of birthing children, and these grain-fed babies were strong and flexible. They bounced when they fell down, physically and emotionally.

In April, 1999, in the final days of my tenth pregnancy, I stopped eating through a petulant fit of impatience, in order to kick-start labor. It seems that when the nutrition dwindles, the body contracts, and this often triggers the birth process. Indeed, within hours, I was having contractions. I had decided to try a hospital midwife, as I was older now. However, the weakening quality of the air and lights in the hospital added to the stress of being so empty and away from my kitchen. Once I arrived at the birth clinic, my contractions completely disappeared. Rather than driving home again, I walked briskly outdoors. It was early April in Alaska, and the snow was not yet completely melted; the wind cut through my clothes like a stabbing knife.

I was soon shivering, but my contractions were responding positively to the fresh cold, finally coming on in stronger waves. I skulked behind bushes (concerned that a nurse would see me and insist I come back indoors) until I couldn't feel my fingers anymore Finally, gratefully, once the labor was back in progress, I walked with difficulty back indoors. Four hours later, David Liam came squalling into our world, handsome then as now.

Once my attention relaxed and the adrenalin started to drain, I found that I was ravenous, almost faint. I surveyed the hospital menu forlornly, twice, before calling home with an emergency order for more food. There was all of nothing in that entire venerable institution that I dared to eat, in my sensitive state. When fresh food was trucked in by my family, I ate it all and hungered for more. Note to hospital staffs everywhere: please consider well-cooked natural foods meals as a vital piece of your positive recovery outcomes. When one is vulnerable in the hospital, food matters most.

After Liam, my tenth child and eighth son, I was determined to have a baby girl the next time. I read somewhere in the old books of macrobiotic folklore that if a mother's condition at conception is more yin (relaxed, loose, expanded) in comparison to the condition of the father, baby girls happen. If the opposite - mother's condition at conception is more yang (centered, tight, contracted) in comparison to the condition of the father - then a boy will develop. I had to check this theory out! My mission was clear: I must eat more loosely and widely than Ted, and change my condition. So, when I was ready, fertile and ovulating, the flood gates opened: I ate coffee and doughnuts for breakfast, pizza for lunch, chocolate ice cream for dinner. I had to drive the car to town all of the time. I had strange body smells. I dreamt weird dreams. For twelve days, I drank wine, ate cheese sandwiches, munched boxes of cookies. Cooking for the family became a huge, boring chore. No one was very happy with my pathetic attempts at meals. I wasn't really hungry nor did I feel much of anything, I became oddly anesthetized. My appetite for sex dissipated, but I had to force it – because after all, getting knocked up in the midst of this chaos was the whole point!

Luckily, I got pregnant right away. When it was confirmed, I hauled my diet back in to my normal home-cooked grain and veggies fare. My energy levels dropped to a dismal low. That was when the cravings began. I dreamt day and night about chocolate. I physically longed for chocolate. I considered hiding chocolate cookies in my sock drawer. Dreamy chocolate clouds intruded on my activities. Instead of giving in to my overwhelming obsessions, I cooked peanut butter cookies, and popcorn balls with mild grain sweeteners, regularly, for my first trimester. Finally, thankfully, three months later, my energy bounced, my chocolate demons vacated the premises and my cravings disappeared. I was so grateful to have my attention back to real food. (I thought these cravings might never end!)

A few seasons following, our lovely and delicately blonde Ellen Trinity was born out in the woods under the gold June sun, first daughter after seven sons in a row. We'll never know if the folklore is correct, or if chance made it appear so.

Ellen's birth is still my favorite. It was on a summer day in June, 2002. I had felt uncomfortably confined in my house, and wandered outside to breathe the clear air and feel the bright Arctic sun on my face. As usual, I had drunk some salty miso broth and chewed some rice to give me the resilient energy of a long distance runner. Then, I sipped cool tea, waiting for the contractions to gain momentum. I moved slowly, from muskeg bed to muskeg bed, watching the spruce trees, stopping to breathe and moan and then relaxing in the soft mosses. I was looking for strawberries, but it was a bit early in the season and all I found was an old metal bowl left, undoubtedly, by some eager berry pickers in the summer before. I felt a bit like a moose, suffering and stumbling through the oh-so-neutral trees, which neither felt sorry for me, nor worried about me, nor celebrated with me. The wind whistled and the sun shone down, it was just a day in the woods like any other. And then, after some time, Ellen was crowning, and she plopped out right onto a muskeg pillow. I looked up at the billowing clouds and down at the pink baby in my arms. I was overwhelmed with delight and I laughed aloud, my voice floating out into the crackling air and strong sunshine.

I picked Ellen up in my arms, even while the cord was still attached. Limping back to the porch, I found my family looking for me, simultaneously shocked, dismayed and overjoyed. They bundled me up and helped me with the afterbirth and cleanup, before cooking me the ultimate comfort food: fried mochi and wakame miso soup topped with garden greens. It tasted really, really good.

All of my happy babies (thirteen of them!) were nursed for nine - fourteen months, and slowly introduced to solid foods at age six months or so, when their first teeth appear. When they began to eat some solid foods, they usually ate a homemade grain porridge called Baby Kokoh. It was their staple food, along with sweet vegetable purees. Kokoh makes small children strong, adaptable and calm. Every baby is different, but my general rule of thumb is that when a baby's first teeth begin to poke through, we begin to feed them solids … and when their molars come and/or they are walking upright, they no longer need that animal quality milk and are ready to be weaned entirely.

Some babies prefer to eat their kokoh plain, and have their sweet vegetable puree on the side... Some prefer to mix their veggie puree in with their kokoh. Either way, if your baby is eating this combination several times per day, you can relax in the knowledge that they are getting the basic nutrients they need in a digestible, wholesome form.

Another favorite way to feed a baby just beginning to eat solids is to pre-chewed brown rice and other grains for them. This makes the nutrients bio-available to their delicate system by infusing the grain with active healthy microbes. Many traditional cultures practiced this method for thousands of generations. Simply chew up a bite of cooked grain until the complex sugars are released and the mouthful is a sweet ambrosia. Then, spit it out into a bowl, or feed directly to baby on a spoon. Pretend you are a mama swallow. All babies LOVE this method of feeding. Anyone who is willing can do this, but remember that the quality of ones' saliva is directly feeding the baby so ones diet should be relatively clean.

In the womb, the developing baby takes in all that the mother ingests, through her bloodstream. This nutrition becomes a foundational part of the quickly growing new being. The effects of mom's diet becomes magnified, times a thousand, as the infant's lifetime supply of teeth, bones, organ tissues and brain development is being grown at incredible speeds. (Today's choice of food is propelled into a future trajectory that is hard to comprehend.) Nursing gives an infant an invaluable start, and irreplaceable immunity for the rest of their lives. Nursing also passes to the infant all the effects of mom's dietary choices, wise and silly alike, magnified, times ten… Baby's growing and absorbing has slowed down considerably by this time, and yet, he has a smaller body to assimilate with, and also growth is still happening. (Even a few days of injury, for example, makes a noticeable difference in a baby's learning progress and can sidetrack development for a long time.) When weaning, chewing a baby's food is a valuable bridge into the big bad world of digesting ones' own food. And, it also directly passes to the child (through the quality of the saliva) the effects of everything mom is eating.

Thus, for me, the mothering process became an appreciable part of my most intimate conversation with myself. I was able to use the baby pressure to hone my appetite to listen to my body, as well as to my direction. I felt that carrying and nursing a baby was the ultimate cuddling experience… However, it was also an uncompromising mirror of my own condition.

Happy Baby Kokoh

1/2 cup brown rice
1/2 cup whole oat groats
1/2 cup sweet rice
1/2 cup barley
2 cups soybeans
2 cups sesame seeds
3 inch piece of kombu (kelp) sea vegetable
12 cups water

1) Toast the grains in a pan over medium high heat until golden, and starting to smell sweet. Set aside.

2) Toast the soybeans in a pan, or oven, until golden and cracking open. Set aside.

3) Rinse the sesame seeds under cold water and drain in a strainer. Then toast over medium heat until they smell delicious and are popping out of the pan. Combine with the soybeans.

4) Grind the soybeans and sesame seeds together in a hand flour mill, so that they become a course meal. You can store this sesame/soy mixture in a jar, or plastic container. This will last for 4-6 pots of kokoh.

5) Combine the toasted grain and 10 cups of water in a pressure cooker (or 12 cups of water in a heavy boiling pot). Add two handfuls of sesame/soy mixture, as well as a 3 inch piece of kombu. Bring up to pressure (or boil), place a "flame tamer" (heat diffusing pad) under the pot, turn flame to low, and simmer for 50 minutes.

6) For babies who don't have molars yet: While the kokoh is still hot, blend well or grind through a Foley food mill. If you have a toddler who can chew somewhat, serve this porridge whole. Keep kokoh in a bowl in the refrigerator for up to 3 days, heating up baby portions as needed.

Combined with pureed vegetables, this is complete and strenghtening nutrition for a growing baby.

LITTLE PEOPLE

"Children are unpredictable. You never know what inconsistency they're going to catch you in next."
~ Franklin P. Jones, turn of the century reporter

When our search for a homeland brought all the Ionia founding families together in Alaska, it was the wild frontier in my life in many ways… I was twenty-one and had four toddlers. I was wide open to the organic forces of pregnancy and babies coming through, and so the little ones came along every twenty months or so. The rhythms of pregnancy, birth, nursing, pregnancy, birth, nursing, became my mainstay. It fit me like a well worn shoe.

As the children piled up into a handful, my relationship to cooking became the impossible matter of churning out more than three meals each day for this hungry crew…. whole oats porridge for breakfast; sweet vegetables for the baby; miso soup, rice, fried black beans, and steamed greens for lunch; broccoli crowns with lemon dressing for snack; millet porridge for dinner. The next day, cook it all again. My marriage was stormy, and my transition into adulthood stormier, but there was always cooking and the sweet murmurs of children brought up on wholesome foods to keep me company. Katie adores rice with seeds… Jane won't eat squash… Gregory eats faster than lightning… Alex hasn't eaten anything green since last week… Lauden is hungry again… and Ted, father of all these youngsters bravely helped cook and wash dishes by my side.

Ted had a very strict Catholic education, which left him with a strong aversion to those religious views built upon the notion of original sin that must be suppressed with punishment and diligence. He preferred a view of trusting the natural forces within us. He and I shared a vision of children growing up without a day already filled up for them – but rather, that they would have the permission and space to figure life out, for themselves. We thought that little humans must have sensitive antennas: we didn't want to cram them up with too many concentrated, refined foods, nor social pressures to conform, obey, or excel, nor fear-based visions of life. For us, it made sense that plainer foods and life in nature, combined with a consistent invitation to participate - alongside their elders - with life's basic activities and questions, might promote a sharp mind, gentle emotions and healthy body that can pick up subtle signals from the universe: the wind, sun, water, time, natural hunger and sexuality, intuition, innovation, inter-connection and the clearest thinking of the times.

It is now known that people develop their lifelong food loves and foundational world view at an early age. If toddlers are given whole natural foods, every day, they will always have a taste for it. For their entire life, wherever they go, whatever they eat, these whole natural food dishes will always mean home. This is a sure way to create a lasting imprint on the future!

Of course, toddlers usually have their own definite ideas about what they will, or will not, eat. My son Aaron, as a young boy, always ate all his vegetables, yet left much of his grain on his plate. My son Lauden was just the opposite – getting him to eat vegetables was an ongoing challenge. I would fry up rice with plenty of vegetables, and the two of them would proceed to pick out their preferred part of the dish. If any of the children ate some packaged snacks, they would only nibble at their dinner. They couldn't taste it any more because their tongue was anesthetized by the large amounts of salt, oil, and/or simple sugars. As a young mother, I worried over what they ate and struggled to be sure that they were eating enough variety. However, I felt that their ability to digest was also dependent on being relaxed, so making an upsetting scene at meals didn't seem useful either. Keeping the house free of any packaged foods helped immeasurably.

My final two little girls, Rosalie and Juliet, were born in our newly built Longhouse Community Center. They enjoy pointing to the spot where they were born. The Longhouse represents a significant shift in our growth as a community from the relatively sheltered past to the new open era, with much more interface with many outsiders. These two girls are Longhouse girls all the way, never shy, outgoing and friendly to all.

However, we've held a strong line of only natural, whole plant foods in the Longhouse. As a result of the daily drone of these wholesome community meals, the later children's attitudes about food are more relaxed. They eat whole foods effortlessly, not because their mother insists but because it is what people do. When they eat in town, they do it wisely, without tension or rebellion.

Young children always know what is going on in a household. They hold little gauges of the emotional temperature and keep internal videos of the family landscape. It's a horrible truth that every parent must face, sooner or later: that ones' children will copy what you do, not do what you say. Food addictions, loves, hates and habits, as well as emotional patterns, even when hidden well, are always obvious to a child. I notice that my eldest children have food and emotional issues which I can trace back to my earlier years, when they were being raised. Even though I have moved on, they are still stuck with those behaviors (which they inherited directly from me at that time.) Now, they must move past them as well. My younger children are not subject to those same issues, because their parent has moved past those sticky habits. We'll see what they grow into! The good news is that every decade moves us forward, toward our life dream, and ones' progress is also recorded vigilantly by those little sponges we call our children.

Whole natural foods make more sense in the wild. Every August, it is a tradition at Ionia to pack up everyone and everything but the kitchen sink to go camping, and berry picking, somewhere wild and beautiful in the lush berry hills. We feel so lucky to live in the land of bountiful amazing strawberries, purple blueberries, pink salmon berries, juicy watermelon berries, tangy currants and raspberries. We often caravan to the Homer docks to catch a ferry across the bay. We set up many tents and a big camp kitchen, and stay for the better part of a week, rain or shine, jamming berries and jamming music around the fire.

The kids love those wild berries! They spoon jam like pudding, pour raw berries over breakfast oats, burn their fingers frying up crepes with berry filling, and carefully wrap pretty little jars of jelly as gifts for family and friends, near and far.

Wild Berry Jam

1) Simmer the berries with a pinch of salt and large dollop of brown rice syrup for twenty minutes. The juice will pour out of the fruits. Keep adding syrup to taste, until it is sweet enough for you.

2) In a small cup, dilute kuzu (or arrowroot) in water, and stir until completely dissolved.

3) Pour the thickener into the berries, stirring constantly, until translucent and creamy. (The jam will gel as it cools).

4) Pour the hot jam directly into jamming jars. Boil the jars in a water broth for twenty minutes. Remove (with jar tongs) and cool until the seal on each jar is sucked in tightly.

These jams will stay good all winter. Open one up every week for spreading on bread, crepes, cereal and crackers.

Early one August morning, in 1999, as we packed up our van to leave on our annual camping trip, I quickly gave the house a once-over check to be sure we had everything. Everything seemed in order. Two hours down the road, as we boarded the large state ferry, I counted heads, eldest to youngest, as was my habit: John and Katie, Jane and Gregory, Alex and Lauden, Connor and James, baby Liam… wait a minute, where is Aaron? It took all of five minutes to assess that no one had seen Aaron (age seven) since late in the previous evening. It was too late to do much about this oversight, as the boat was leaving the dock and all aboard whose coming aboard! Once we arrived in the sleepy village of Seldovia, we located the ancient phone booth for several panicked phone calls. Aaron was bewildered and sleepy. He sheepishly admitted to staying up late in front of a movie and crawling under the cover of the couch for warmth at four am, like a large lump of cushion. I sheepishly admitted that, in my packing fervor, between the toddler issues and the tween dilemmas, I didn't actually think to look for him until the Homer docks. The following morning, Aaron got his own plane ride to Seldovia, flying low over the sparkling bay before landing jerkily onto the Seldovia Slough, a rough patch of mud water jokingly called the float plane landing area.

In my family, it is an ongoing source of amusement to recount the (handful of) times when I left one of the kids at home, or at a store. In the days before cell phones and text messaging, this was one of the hazards of living in a large, organically disorganized family such as ours. While we had many balls in the air and sometimes one fell down… we chose to lean toward trusting children and their ability to take care of themselves and learn common sense, rather than too much pampering, control, or strict authority.

When my sons Gregory and Alex first began to cook meals, at age eight or nine, they could only watch one pot at time. First, they would put on the brown rice, then play cards while watching the timer for forty minutes. Then they would begin to work on the soup… boil beans, dice vegetables… and once the soup was finished, they would begin to think about vegetable side dishes. We tried several times to show them a more efficient approach, however, they soon lost interest. It became slowly clear that young, beginning cooks have their own unique pathways into love of cooking. The boys were better off left to master the kitchen in their own manner. They are now excellent, self assured cooks.

We didn't school the kids in any conventional manner. The older kids cared for the younger ones. They all absorbed basic farm, family and community skills, including the ability to listen, and communicate with people of all ages. As young adults, they follow their interests unconditionally, a few of them at top universities. However, it has been hard for them in many ways to transition into modern, competitive cultural norms. They were built for community.

Kids at Ionia (and indeed, most of the kids I've seen who eat whole natural foods) are, overall, smart and happy, robust and sweet hearted. My idealism for their future has melded in the fire of daily life and daily discussion, mellowed by our setbacks and disappointments, into a quiet determination to grow into a true multi-generational village… I want more than anything to provide these kids, and the kids to come, with a livable, integrated, wholesome alternative to the disconnects we so often find in contemporary society. In the process, I have learned how to cook. Apparently, sometimes, this is what it takes.

FINDING COMPANY AND SOURCING INGREDIENTS

"Change will not come if we wait for some other person, or if we wait for some other time. We are the ones we've been waiting for. We are the change that we seek." ~ *President Barack Obama*

My mother didn't plan my arrival into this world, but when I came along she took the responsibility of child raising seriously and was forever searching for a way to bring me up that made more sense to her. I attended a multitude of different schools based on numerous educational philosophies: Montessori, Steiner, "free", Catholic, as well as American public schools. They each contributed a bit of something to my world view - however, at none of these schools did I learn how to cook, or eat. Finally, in the fifth grade, my parents pulled me out of schools altogether and decided to teach me at home. I was unschooled from then on and taught myself in the topics that interested me: design, writing, sewing… and cooking. This was the beginning of really "seeing" food, or caring about its implications to my life.

In 1970, like the addict who is starting a new life, clean and sober, my mother started our new macrobiotic diet by cleaning out our cupboards and refrigerators, radically changing our environments, making new friends and leaving some old ones behind. We packed up everything that contained refined sugars, chemicals, strong spices, additives, margarine, and threw it away as no longer fit to be consumed. We made a thoughtful decision about animal foods, including dairy and eggs. (This is a very personal choice built on deeply held points of view.) We stocked up with whole, fresh ingredients (beans, grains, seeds, nuts, vegetables and fruits) and natural organic seasonings (sea salt, shoyu, miso, a few herbs, whole grain syrups, unrefined oils and vinegars.) We immersed ourselves in the culture and values of whole foods and natural medicine: learned simple home remedies, exercised in nature, stopped using modern pharmaceuticals. Our interest in whole foods spilled out toward creating community, environmental and social justice, organic growing, natural building and clothing.

In my later years, I have seen more and more households making the change gradually to whole foods, like slowly revitalizing inner city neighborhoods. One by one, new and strange dishes are showing up on the tables across America: quinoa…miso soup…steamed kale. A fruit compote. Inevitably like the turning tide, the old habits and food addictions in countless families have started to fall away: the chocolate syrup looks sickly, the powdered mashed potatoes taste stale and the canned goods give way to their fresher cousins.

It seems that changing ones diet is bigger than changing ones religion. Good luck, it's a long, sometimes lonely road, but there are many beautiful sights along the way. Like born again evangelists, we often push our families to change their diets as well - either in a desperate bid for social support, or worry for the health of those we love. These types of efforts are usually met with mirth, irritation and finally, serious push back. No one appreciates being scolded about the chocolate chip muffin on their breakfast table, and will usually defend it vehemently.

In my life, our food changes defined who we were as a family. My grandparents resented that we couldn't eat out just anywhere or more importantly, share in their family dinners. This put undeniable distance between us. When presented with a brief explanation of my family's food limits, other parents would sometimes defend themselves quite vehemently from perceived attack, which was awkward. Once, my husband and I attended a big family reunion dinner at a swanky seafood restaurant in Florida. My mother-in-law had been so supportive of our diet, she went the extra mile to make sure we had the foods we needed. She even joined us in our meals. However, that night I decided to throw myself into the spirit of celebration and eat a salmon smothered with crème sauce accompanied by a glass of chardonnay and chocolate raspberry cake. I could practically hear the sigh of relief around the table from the various relatives, it seemed that my simple salad choices had previously been quite a source of social tension.

My kids couldn't accept lollipops from the bank tellers; join many other kids' social food activities; buy popcorn or drinks at the movies or gyms; go trick or treating, or for holiday meals, at anyone else's home. We lived on an island, a different culture of food.

Once, I brought all my kids to the local county fair on the Kenai Peninsula. We saw the giant cabbages and the jumbo pigs. We rode festive ponies in a circle, and rickety roller coasters, and we bought corn on the cob. We sat down at the picnic tables to eat our packed lunch from home: grain corn, sautéed daikon radish greens and watermelon. As we ate, a middle-aged, big fellow with a stubble of a red beard sidled up beside me, pointedly gestured at my bowl and asked, loudly, "What's that?" I answered him, politely yet rather distractedly, "corn and sautéed greens". I hoped that he would wander away and leave us be. "That is corn" he informed me firmly, waving at my corn on the cob, "But what's that?" and his finger came perilously close to burying itself in my bowl of grain corn. At this juncture, I considered launching into a biting lecture about the inadvisability of touching strangers' lunches, but, at the last moment, I decided that he was merely curious, and perhaps a little drunk. So, I explained sweetly that this, too, was corn, dried and stored as a grain, rather than eaten fresh as a vegetable. He listened intently, and then smiled and repeated my words, except in his version: "So that corn was dried up because it didn't have any rain?" I tried several different descriptions, but I don't think it ever really made it over the wall of sense to this poor fellow. By the time we got through the explanation of sautéed daikon radish greens he was thoroughly out of his element, and the kids were irritated by this underlining of our out-of-place-ness.

Living in Alaska, we rarely eat tropical fruit because it is grown "so far from home". One day in the market, my eight year old daughter Jane pointed to a banana in the cart in front of us and asked loudly, "What is that?" Everyone in line turned and stared, disapprovingly, at us. The attention wasn't all negative: one time, five sons, one by one, bought little bags of nuts and raisins, and the teller asked me earnestly "How do you get your kids to eat raisins? My kids hate them." I was often told how well spoken and well behaved my threadbare throng of children were. My standard reply was, "Well, we don't eat sugar."

Somewhere along the way, I discovered the bliss of keeping the environment at home totally free of store-bought snacks, then trusting the children's appetites within that environment. However, all of my kids, at one time or another, when they came of a certain age, rode their dirt bikes the six miles down the country road to the little gas station convenience store to buy some candy, chips. or a soft drink. Of course, they never told me about it; and I pretended innocence to let them have some autonomy. It was pretty easy to spot – their behavior became quite speeded up and oddly aggressive. Their ears turned bright red and they slept fitfully, sometimes even developing a fever, sore throat or headache. Hopefully, they noticed it too.

I got in the habit of scouring menus and buffets for anything whole and simple. In 2008, a small group of us from Ionia attended a six day national mental health conference, called Alternatives, which was held in Omaha, Nebraska that year. The conference was located in a fabulous hotel complex in lovely downtown Omaha, which had recently been totally refurbished for us tourists. There were no kitchens which we could access anywhere. We were surrounded by marble hallways with fountains, pigs in a blanket, gourmet coffees and champagne bars, with no edible food in sight. There wasn't even a vegan salad on the menu. After the first 24 hours, all we had from home was some stale cornbread we had steamed in jars. I had a few moments of panic at the prospect of living on non-sugar soy lattes and dry toast for the next six days. In our hotel rooms, however, were coffee machines, a means of heating water. With our food kits from home, we proceeded to make a quick miso broth with scallions and dulse (seaweed) for our breakfasts. And we scoured the local neighborhood for food we could relate to. Happily, we did find a little Indian restaurant which served vegan entrees: it was heavy on the curries, but included rice and beans and flat breads. That took care of our dinners. Then, in a small corner mart next to the cola and stale baloney sandwiches, we found a refreshing and clean bean salad, clearly locally made. It was made with olive oil, sweet red peppers, cilantro, onions and salt. We filled our little hotel room fridges up with bean salads, and ate those with our cornbread for the rest of the week. Thank you, Omaha!

The aisles of the supermarket are full, but I no longer walk down most of those aisles, because I have no expectation of finding real food here. Ted calls it dancing down the aisles of Safeway. The whole foods ingredients are few and far between, tucked into only a few of the shelves, here and there. I find some organic pastas and jams, brown rice, dry beans and produce in-between the colas, the white breads and the cans of sugared up vegetables. In the long search for cultural company about food, there has been lots of baklava, sushi, burritos or falafels from the local ethnic joints; as well as exploratory stops at farmers markets, salad bars, juice bars and expensive organic food shops and cafes.

The obvious emerging solution for the ingredients crisis and social crisis was to gather with like-minds to create a food buying cooperative, which enabled us to purchase goods in bulk, at wholesale prices. Buying cases of organic kale, gallons of shoyu and sunflower oil, 25 # bags of millet and sesame seeds, etc., allows our pantry to affordably fill up with the basics. Sharing this practical resource with other families gives us some vital company.

These are our favorite online stores for bulk whole foods:

- NATURAL IMPORT
- GOLD MINE NATURAL FOODS
- UNITED NATURAL FOODS INC
- SUZANNES SPECIALTIES

The dream is to farm our own local grain, beans and seeds, harvest, ferment and preserve gardens and orchards, wild berries, sea vegetables and wild greens. We have to fallow off the old food paradigm, cultivate new thinking, and develop modern ways of living that support these subsistence activities. I am discovering that it is also a regional effort and a grass roots movement. This seems to happen slowly, yet surely, over several generations.

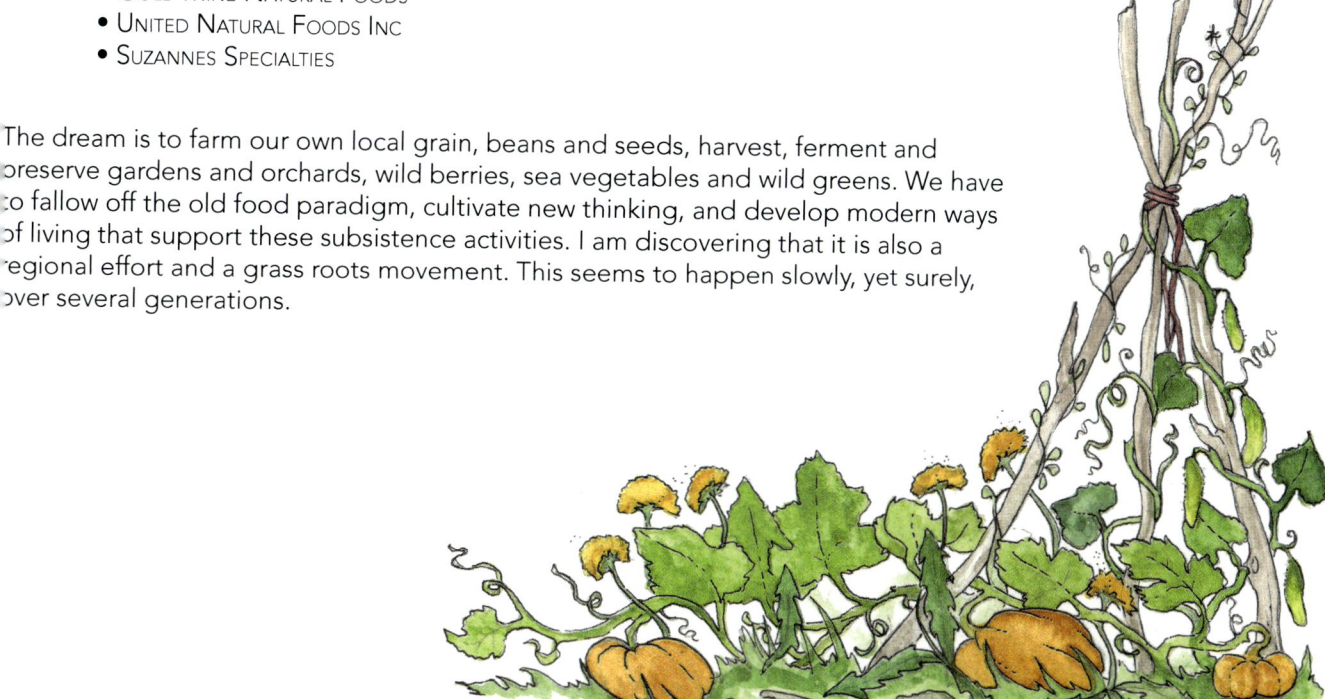

ILLNESS, INJURY, AND HOME REMEDIES

"We are all failures - at least the best of us are."
~ J.M. Barrie, Scottish author and dramatist

Over the thirty years of raising kids, there have of course been many fevers, coughs, colds, sore throats, rashes, infections, earaches, headaches, body-aches, stomachaches (and various other mysterious illnesses) in our household. Sometimes in Alaska's mid-winter, long and devastating flus sweep through. These illnesses are seen as temporary guests, not necessarily invited, yet serving a useful purpose in our life. Illness and inflammation trigger a discharge of any excess held deep in our bodies, like squeezing toothpaste out of a tube. We view this as nature's way of preventing more serious dis-ease further down the road. However, no one enjoys being sick and even "healthy discharges" (or de-tox's) can grow tiresome, painful or threatening. When I want to treat or sooth these symptoms, here are some of my favored home remedies. These have worked for us, but I am not a health expert or a trained macrobiotic counselor - and each situation and family is unique - so it is essential that each person relies on their own judgement (and health professionals, as needed) for keeping well.

MEDICINES FROM THE KITCHEN:

KUZU is a powdered, processed root of a thickly growing vine sometimes called kudzu. It is most often used similarly to corn starch, to thicken or gel sauces, desserts, and stews. Kuzu drinks are also used as a very healing medicine, strengthening for our intestines, the source of immunity. When the gut is healthy, all else follows. Kuzu drinks are soothing and relaxing, settling and gathering all at the same time. Salty kuzu drinks are great for an overly expanded or acidic condition (nausea, diarrhea). Sweet kuzu drinks are better in cases where the person is quite contracted (unable to sleep, with a dry cough or a pounding headache.)

MISO is a fermented, salty, cooking paste from Asia which is often used to season a nourishing broth, chock full of micro-organisms whose job is to create a healthy bio-sphere in your gut. If you need to take in pharmaceutical medications or radiation, miso broth (with a bit of wakame seaweed added in) is especially beneficial for recovery. After a round of antibiotics, for example, I am sure to drink some miso broth with wakame every day for ten days.

UMEBOSHI, the traditional Japanese pickled plum, has a dynamic quality of sour, sweet and salty which seems to have miraculous healing qualities. Umeboshi is wonderful for whenever I am feeling "off".

Remedies for Common Illnesses:

1) HOT BATH: Relief for most everything, excepting a fever.

2) UME-SHOYU-KUZU DRINK: To treat nausea, stomach aches, diarrhea, or hangovers. Combine half of an umeboshi plum and 1 teaspoon of shoyu in 1 1/2 cups of water. Simmer for 5 minutes. Dissolve 2 teaspoons of kuzu in cold water, pour into the simmering liquid, stirring constantly for about 2 minutes, until it becomes clear and viscous. Drink while warm.

3) MISO BROTH: For nourishment during all sorts of flus, chills, ear and throat infections; when tired, stressed, or depleted; and for stimulating the appetite. Simmer an inch of kombu (kelp) in water for 10 minutes. Turn off the flame, dissolve miso in the soup to taste and drink while warm.

4) APPLE JUICE KUZU: To help release headaches, locked up backs or necks; to bring on sleep; for relaxing irritation and restlessness; and to soothe dry, hacking coughs. Simmer organic apple juice for 5 minutes. Dissolve 2 teaspoons of kuzu in cold water, pour into the simmering liquid, stirring constantly for 2 minutes, until clear and viscous. Drink while warm.

5) SALT WATER WASH: For clearing up eye infections, gum infections, or infected splinters; for temporary relief of sore throats; and to disappear some skin rashes.

6) UMEBOSHI PLUM TEA: To relieve most any mild illness or poisoning, inflammation, acidity or crankiness. Simmer 1 umeboshi plum in 2 cups of water for 10 minutes. Dissolve the plum with your spoon and drink everything while warm.

7) GRATED RAW, GREEN SOUR APPLE IN HOT WATER: To relax a locked up neck or back; for help releasing headaches; for relieving after-birth cramps; and for stimulating the appetite of a child who won't eat.

8) TEA FROM WILD CHAMOMILE AND YARROW: To settle upset stomachs; strengthen the digestive tract; soothe flus and infections.

9) SHOYU TEA: To snap back to center when feeling feint, dizzy, nauseous or weak; for when everything tastes awful; or for fast energy. Sprinkle a handful of kukicha (tea twigs) into 2 cups boiling water. Add 1 T of shoyu (salty!), drink while hot.

10) CABBAGE LEAF POULTICE: For cooling fevers, swelling and inflammation. Place fresh green cabbage leaves directly onto the inflamed or hot area, and replace regulary as they become limp.

Children who have fevers or colds are not happy eaters. Often a young child or elderly person will lose a lot of weight while sick. This is natural, but sometimes worrisome. Softly cooked brown rice "kayu" cream, with umeboshi plum, is highly digestible nourishment, very lulling and palliative for sick bodies, for after surgery, or for anytime normal food is not possible.

If a small child - or anyone really - gets too tight and too malnourished, they will sometimes lose their appetite altogether. It's as if their body forgets that eating is life giving, and delicious. In this case, I always expand the offerings to include apple sauce, raw watermelon and other juicy fruit, carrot juice, udon noodles in a mild broth, anything that will trigger their system to relax and expand.

Babies and toddlers need very little salt in their daily fare, if any. As they grow, they can tolerate more and more, however children who are sick need to eat very clean and plain food, with less oil and salt than usual. Occasionally, if one of my kids eats too much salt, they will get muscle cramps in their legs. Or, they will grind their teeth at night. A hot bath will remedy these difficult symptoms. On the opposite side of the spectrum, when my kids eat sugar or too much fruit juice, they will often come down with a fever or sore throat, or cry and throw unreasonable fits about nothing and everything all day, or hurt themselves repeatedly. This is typical over-sugared behavior, and will burn off with time.

In my search for a life in which my family's health is more in the hands of nature, I think that I often erred over to the "do nothing" philosophy of healing. This has mostly worked well enough. I have seen children with very high fevers ride them out with no lasting harm. Some cool cabbage leaves, applied directly to the child's forehead, can be helpful for lowering temperatures, and feels great. My son Alex once had a fever which just kept rising, no matter what we tried. When it hit 104 degrees I panicked and sent Ted down a snowy road in the middle of the night for medication. By the time the meds arrived, the fever had spiked, and was on its way down. While I do feel that over-use of pharmaceuticals can be devastating to our innate strength and ability to heal, all medicines, when used prudently and wisely, earn their place in the family toolbox. I am so thankful to modern medications for being there for that bladder infection which just won't go away, or for that time when six year old Liam ate fifty sheets of dried nori at one sitting (as a dare?) which blocked up his stomach… Or for when Ellen's swine flu became pneumonia, and we couldn't turn it around with milder, natural approaches.

HEALING RICE KAYU CREME

2 cups short grain brown rice
1 umeboshi plum
16 cups water

1) Combine all ingredients in a pressure cooker or heavy-lidded boiling pot.

2) Bring up to pressure (or high boil), turn flame to low and place a flame tamer under the pot so that the rice slowly simmers for 1 1/2 hours.

3) When the pressure cooker is down from pressure, grind the soft and creamy porridge through a Foley food mill, discarding the rice hulls. Alternatively, blend into a creme.

While it is best served fresh, you can keep rice kayu creme in a cold spot for up to a week, but always serve hot.

Rice Kayu Creme is so soothing when you are feeling sick, especially with a little umeboshi.

Growing up wild in our Alaska homestead also brought along many injuries. My boys and girls are known for tumbling down a snowy ravine (John Emrys), crashing over homemade snow-board jumps (Gregory), chopping at his finger with an axe (Aaron), burning and cutting themselves while cooking (everybody). With thirteen active kids, we have seen too many cuts, mild burns, bruises, and sprains to remember, and even a few broken bones, concussions and deep burns. For serious injuries, the medical know-how and technology of a hospital is hard to replace.

One summer afternoon, when Connor was eight months old, he napped peacefully in my tipi as I cut firewood on a chopping block outside. I could hear him gurgle and coo as he woke up, but kept on swinging my axe. Suddenly, he was screaming. I rushed inside to find him crawling his way out of the cold, ash filled fire pit. Connor's little foot had sunk way down, under the top layer of ash, into hidden hot coals buried below. The tender skin was burned away.

I treated this severe burn as I had treated milder burns always: with cool water, aloe vera, and a daily wrap of comfrey leaves. After ten days, Connor's foot had healed up perfectly, into a knotted fist of scar tissue… Instead of toes, he now had a clubfoot. I cried and cried in regret and sorrow. We immediately brought him in to our nearest clinic to survey the damages and see what could be done. After a few weeks of preparation and consultation, a plastic surgeon was able to surgically separate Connor's toes and graft skin from his belly onto the bottom of his foot. This is how I learned, the hard way, that third degree burns may need skin-grafting in order to heal correctly! Conner's foot has hairy, tender skin, but we are grateful every day that he can walk.

Thus, keying into ones' intuition about when to stay home, and when to run in to the hospital, is important. In less extreme cases, a few well placed remedies can work miracles.

Remedies for Common Injuries:

1) **FOR BURNS:** soak in cool water for a long time, until the heat settles down. Then, spread on aloe vera gel OR sesame oil. Fresh local honey is also amazing antibiotic therapy for burns that may infect. Wash every day with salt water, then replace the honey ointment.

2) **FOR SWELLING, SPRAINS AND BRUISES:** cabbage leaf poultice. Hold the leaf directly on the swollen area until it wilts. Replace and repeat until there is some relief.

3) **FOR BEE, SPIDER OR ANT STINGS:** spit on tobacco and place it directly on the sting. Alternatively, yarrow flowers work well also.

4) **FOR WOUNDS:** I use a salve made from beeswax and medicinal herbs. Dried nori (seaweed) makes an excellent healing bandage because it has skin healing properties, and contracts as it dries (holding the wound together). To remove the nori bandage, simply soak the wound in warm water.

5) **FOR DISAPPEARING SCARS,** place soaked kelp directly onto the scar tissues for an hour (or as long as you can) each day. Seaweed is famously good for skin.

In the fall of 2011, I accompanied Ted and friends to a Natural Building Colloquium held out in the woods of an Oregon camp. At this gathering, I cooked for a group of twelve of us every day, but on the final evening, I joined the staff in their celebration chocolate cake and coffee. It was fun, however I could taste the intense corn syrup, eggs and cheap oil foreign to my system.

Once we returned home, I mysteriously came down with shingles, a terrible virus related to chicken-pox, which generates a vicious skin rash and stinging nerves. This was the most disturbing pain I have ever experienced. It felt like the layer under my skin was on fire. I was pacing and jumping in agony, and Ted rushed me to the emergency room where they quickly diagnosed me, gave me their strongest pain narcotic and anti-viral medications. However, they informed us that shingles has no known cure, can last for weeks, months, and, sometimes, never fully disappear!

I was desperate. Upon returning home, I read up on the anti-viral meds, deciding, finally, not to try them out because they appeared to have big risks and doubtful benefits. However, I faithfully took my pain medications. But the narcotics didn't work. I couldn't sleep, nor sit still. I finally ran a bath, and filled it with seaweed. I sat in the mineral-y water up to my neck. The heat was the wrong direction - it irritated my skin rash into a frenzy. So, I soaked several long strands of alaria kelp in cold water, stripped off all of my clothes and wrapped myself in the seaweed, like a second skin. It was heavenly relief! I could breathe. I could think. I lay on my bed, naked, wrapped in cool seaweed fronds, like a mermaid. My skin rash was so hot that we had to change out the kelp often, but luckily we had our large annual supply stored in the root cellar. Slowly, yet without doubt, the rash cooled out, retreated, and finally disappeared over the next thirty hours. The stinging never returned. It was a healing seaweed miracle!

The founders of Ionia chose not to immunize our children, in the belief that our natural immunity would make us stronger as a people, in the long run. Therefore, we have experienced many influxes of infectious illnesses, from chicken pox to whooping cough. They are hard, but everybody recuperated completely. Every one of the babies experience rubella soon after being weaned, and we've come to see it as a natural process of throwing off the animal proteins from mother's milk, an aid to growing up. We utilize our tried and true home remedies, and watch carefully for full recovery, with the view that we are host to a complex network of microbes which sustain us, and that we are incredibly resilient and adaptable.

Mothers, by definition, worry. It's part of the position description. For balance, its good to meditate on the thought that every difficulty can serve a purpose, and every front has a back. Kids get sick and kids get hurt, sometimes seriously. It is often a natural part of growing up, and it is part of getting stronger. Three of my children lived through serious burns or illnesses when they were quite small, and I am amazed to see that they are the wisest and most compassionate of all.

My friend Bill (Johnson) has a wonderful way of reminding me of the macrobiotic view that every front has a back, and the bigger the front, the bigger the back – and there is really no such thing as health and sickness…. There is only the adventure of life's ups and downs… and over the hill of feeling better is feeling worse… and around the corner is feeling better again. When you have some health, you spend it, and when you have some illness, you save up to overcome it. If you are born strong, you abuse your body because you can, and if you are born weak, you are careful and prudent with your choices. When you hurt yourself, or get into trouble, you slow down and wise up. And so it goes, throughout your lifetime… Food is just a tool to play with, to cook up your next adventure.

chapter four

COOKING

THE CENTERED KITCHEN

"Quiet the mind, and the soul will speak."
~ Ma Jaya Sati Bhagavati, spiritual teacher from New York City

Once, I attempted to cook meals in a hotel kitchen in India. I was surrounded by male chefs, chattering in Hindi, who sautéed up spicy pans of oily rice and beans over smoky hot, flaming burners. The heavy hot air, mixed with outgassing propane, hung in the kitchen like a blanket; the dirty counters were cluttered with bags and bottles of ingredients that felt as if they had been sitting there since the twenties. Cockroaches and ants enjoyed the leftovers from yesterday scattered on the cracked floor. The sink was full of oily galvanized metal dishes, all of the time. These guys were incredible chefs, and they cranked out amazing, spicy meals, day in and day out, however I was paralyzed in that environment, unable to cook a single dish that was very good. My meals were a disaster.

Having a kitchen which I love, and even respect, is a vital part of my love of cooking. My kitchen can be a sanctuary of self-esteem and self-support. Whether it is a pint-sized tipi kitchen, or a full-fledged community kitchen, if I take care of the space then it takes care of me. This is my haven and my comfort place. I create a large counter space and plenty of shelving to keep gallon jars of dry goods, favorite cooking pots and bowls. An oversized cutting board that can easily hold a few bunches of greens and a handful of carrots is valuable. Gas or wood fired burners are a necessity.

Often, modern kitchens are stuff magnets: everyone's miscellaneous stuff - from mail to keys, medications to cds, books, magazines, sweaters and hats, toys - it all ends up resting on the kitchen table. What a hazard to the cooking process! For me to cook, all this must go - it must find another home, somewhere. I kick it out and proclaim the kitchen a clutter free zone. Once a month, I deep clean the kitchen for a few hours. If my kitchen is free of clutter, clean and organized and I more or less know where everything goes, my mind becomes less cluttered as well, and more receptive to discovering new things and cooking with intention.

I always own a balanced, sharp vegetable cutting knife, which I sharpen briefly each time I reach for it. (I like the kitchen knives from the on-line store, Japanese Woodworker.) Handling my knife, as a treasured tool, is part of cooking's subtle pleasures. When life feels like I am simply running from one emergency to the next, it is hard to tune into one's knife, yet cutting techniques call for attention. Closing the door of the kitchen, not conversing, and putting some intention into being present not only helps my mental well being, and the meal taste better, but helps with the rest of the day's pressures as well.

Each meal is a chance to hone my cutting techniques. I hold the knife firmly, yet not too tightly. I am mindful of the knife's angle and learn to tuck my finger tips away from the blade, even when I am moving quickly. I let the knife's weight do most of my cutting, rather than my muscles. Each year, my slicing is thinner, quicker and more elegant. Cutting in many shapes and sizes helps to make meals dynamic and pleasing.

When setting up a kitchen, besides lots and lots of counter space, there are a few cooking utensils which I have found to be quite indispensable:

- sharp, comfortable vegetable cutting knife with a stainless or porcelain blade

- stainless steel (not aluminum) pressure cooker

- porcelain ginger grater

- wire mesh hand held strainer

- large sturdy colander

- long handled bamboo or wooden stirring spoons

- suribachi (serrated, porcelain mortar with wooden pestle)

- stainless or cast iron sauté pot with a tight fitting lid in an appropriate size for the household

- stainless soup pot with glass or stainless lid that fits well

- agreeable mixing bowls in several sizes

- glass jars for storing grains, beans, and seeds

- two flame tamers (metal heat diffusers used under pots)

- pint and quart glass jars are useful for many things from storing dry goods and leftovers, to drinking tea

- gas or wood fires are the best sources of heat - electric is less desirable and microwave is unacceptable

MENU DESIGN

"Peace begins in the kitchens and pantries, gardens and backyards, where our food is grown and prepared. The energies of nature and the infinite universe are absorbed through the foods we eat, and are transmuted into our thoughts and actions." ~ Michio Kushi, grandfather of macrobiotics

The best cooking is the simplest. Whole, fresh ingredients, cooked plainly, are some of life's most enjoyable pleasures. To be able to serve a meal of sweet vegetable millet with blanched kale, you must be a very confident cook. The confidence comes from the love of the foods. To learn to cook without recipes, one must find the appetite for simple dishes. If this appetite is missing, it is easy to find: simply water fast for a full day, and it will appear, like magic.

Harvesting, preparing and cooking takes time, and most people these days don't have any. At most homes I know which are dependent on home cooked meals of real ingredients, a cooking schedule springs up. At my house, by necessity, the kids cook from a young age, and the teens are capable and even sensational cooks. My partner cooks. My housemates cook. Extended family cooks. My community members cook. Everyone cooks. It is unrealistic for any one person to cook all three meals each day all the time, unless they are super mom, and I find this expectation disturbing. As home-cooked meals become the only edible food around, sharing cooking shifts becomes one of life's essentials, like paying bills.

For me, the hardest part of cooking is planning the menu. What to cook, what to cook today? Planning must happen around the food available: First the grain is chosen, and the beans and vegetable dishes spiral out from that. I find that the choice of grain sets the tone for the meal.

At my home, we usually eat brown rice once each day, because it is easy to chew well and very centering. For variety, I love brown rice with barley (soothing and bouncy), rice with wheat (so sweet), rice with aduki beans or other beans (rich and pretty), or rice with grain corn (so satisfying to my American soul). The other meals in the day will be built around contrasting grains like millet, polenta or buckwheat. In the occasional dinner, grain is the main part of a one-pot meal – such as a sweet barley porridge with many vegetables.

For breakfasts, I often cook a quick pot of miso soup. For something a little more substantial, we will make a whole grain porridge: barley, rice, whole oats or buckwheat, or sometimes, polenta or cracked oats. The porridge is eaten plain, or with a topping of toasted sesame seeds, tahini, shoyu, sweet white miso, or brown rice syrup.

CREAMY OATS

1) At night, bring 1 cup of oats to a boil with 6 cups of water and a pinch of salt. Let it sit all night with a cover.

2) In the morning, add a bit more water if need be, and carefully bring up to boil again on a medium flame (stirring to prevent burning).

3) Lower the flame to very low, add a "flame tamer" heat diffusing pad, and simmer for 15 minutes. If you like, add a handful of raisins, bubble for a few more minutes, then serve.

Alternatively, add the oats to the cold water and pinch of salt, place the pot on TWO heat pads over a very low flame, all night long.

Whole oat porridge is a favorite kids' breakfast, and a deeply satisfying alternative to rolled oats (which can sometimes taste much like cardboard.) I usually make soups every day, but not every meal. Everyone loves soup. It is an easy way to assimilate nutrients and, therefore, is comforting. That salty broth is, perhaps, deeply reminiscent of the ocean, or of the womb. Soup warms your stomach, stimulates your appetite and is a nourishing way to take in liquid. Miso soup, clear shoyu broths, creamy vegetable or bean soups are all useful and sublime.

Whole grains, beans and vegetables are cooked with lots of liquid, so drinking becomes less important ... It's very easy to stay hydrated, especially if you aren't eating dried and baked chips and crackers. When you do crave something to drink, natural herbal teas, preferably the less stimulating versions, are a satisfying addition to many meals. Kukicha tea (which is the twigs of the tea plant) is comforting and harmonizing with most meals and desserts; chamomile tea is relaxing and rejuvenating; raspberry and mint are refreshing; chaga, yarrow and nettle have wonderful healing qualities. Fresh wild or domestic herbs growing outside are the tastiest and best for you – however, dried is convenient and abundantly available.

Vegetable and bean dishes vary with the seasons, my mood and time constraints. When cooking whole foods without recipes the variety becomes endless and infinitely subtle. The meal's design depends on what's in the pantry today, and what signals are coming through the cook.
Simple meals are wonderful:
- brown rice, nori and blanched carrots with sesame seeds
- soba noodles in broth with sautéed napa cabbage

More filled out meals are also tremendous:
- clear broth soup with mushrooms and green onions, sweet vegetable millet, lima-bean-root-veggie stew, blanched carrot, kale-and-radish salad with lemon dressing, and stewed apples with pecans
- kidney-bean-rice, toasted sunflower seeds, miso soup with wakame, carrot- squash nishime*, fresh hiziki (sea vegetable) salad

It's amazing how many different meals can emerge from the ingredients in the pantry. Each dish is never quite the same as any other, but themes and favorite combinations emerge. I have started to listen to the weather, the environment as well as the food itself - What do these gorgeous fresh green onions or limp celery stalks have to say about what to cook today? A snowstorm blows me toward a warming, hearty stew; or a visitor from Guatemala conjures up visions of tamales; or the spring dandelion greens are calling out to be included in the meal. I usually want lighter, fresher dishes in the heat, and warming, centering dishes in the cold - except when I don't, as there are exceptions to every rule. Celebrations are an excuse to go all out and cook something really elaborate. In my young mothering days, lavish holiday cooking with friends and family were my favorite... Now, as I settle into middle age, my favorite cooking moments are alone in a quiet kitchen with a few root vegetables.

Whether poor or rich in ingredients, a cook who listens to her/his intuition is listening to the infinite itself. The power of the whole food is streaming through the cooking utensils onto the plates. It is a basic raw and unadorned biological power. With whole grains at the center, one can't really go wrong. I feel that much of my family's destiny is in my hands at that moment, being co-created every day, day in day out, with the daily meal. It is an honorable and influential position.

*see page 75 for a description of nishime

COOKING FORCES

"There is no sincerer love than the love of food." ~ *George Bernard Shaw*

A hot, home-cooked meal prepared from scratch with fresh ingredients is going to be the most attractive food around. No matter how amazing or addictive a packaged food can be, it is not as delicious as home-cooked fare. The aromas of home-baked bread, or squash recently out of the oven, the sizzle of sautéed greens, a rich steaming kidney bean stew, an original savory noodle broth honed to perfection with the garnish on hand, these are the meals that sweet memories are made of. Taken a step further, home-made ingredients and condiments such as pickles from all cultural traditions, tofu and tempeh, seitan and mochi, miso, vinegars and sake, jams and butters are so superior to the store-bought variety that, sometimes, they inspire spontaneous cheers in their honor. And so they should: the dedicated cooks who create these treats are salient contributors to our quality of life. The cook keeps everyone coming back for more.

Cooking changes the energy of raw foods using fire, water, time, fermentation and by combining. By manipulating these forces, we significantly change the energy of foods we eat. Whole food that is cooked well is very delicious, satisfying and gives us lots of energy. The energy within the cooking releases the good tastes in the foods. Balanced cooking also makes the nutrients bio-available and highly digestible.

Gathering together one's tools - the forces of fire, water, time, fermentation - cooking becomes a practical art, a dance with infinity.

FIRE AND TIME: Uncooked dishes are cooling and cleansing. An entire diet in which most of the fare is raw might, at first, feel appropriate and liberating (especially after a lifetime of heavy animal proteins.) However, over time, this is likely to create chronic weakness. On the other hand, a diet in which much of the fare is popped, scorched, dehydrated, blackened, braised or crispy could at first feel galvanizing, but, over time will likely create chronic tightness. Use time wisely in cooking: long, slow cooked dishes create the deeper flavors, strength and sturdiness...quick cooked dishes, over a high flame, create crunch, radiance and pep.

WATER: Generally, wetter dishes (porridges, stews, soups, softer sloppier beans) are more relaxing and softening. I find soups to be a wonderful way to relax my system. However if every dish is watery, over time, the overall effect of the diet will be loosening and weakening. On the other hand, dryer dishes (chewable, fluffy grains, flaky beans, harder sinewy veggies) are more gathering and contracting. Chewy brown rice has a uniquely centering effect on my system. If every dish is dry, however, the overall effect of the diet, over time, will be hardening and withering.

FERMENTATION: The process of fermentation is the cook collaborating with nature to make whole foods thoroughly nourishing and satisfying. Your belly desperately needs the forest of healthy microbial action - bacteria, fungi, archaea and the enzymes they create - which the process of fermenting feeds. Our intestines communicate with our brain constantly and thousands of astonishing microbes live there, governing our health and happiness. For this reason, every traditional cooking method includes some form of fermented foods : miso, shoyu, umeboshi, vinegars, sauerkraut, pickles, sourdough, tempeh, beer, yogurt, stink heads, pickled eggs, cheeses, etc. In the modern diet, live fermentation is very rare. Without those little critters, our insides are operating with a severe debilitating handicap. A smart cook makes friends with these micro-organisms and invites them into meals often. It is a vital touch for the overall.

COMBINING: Combining whole foods ingredients without using an understanding of balance is usually unappetizing. I have experienced that the worst and best cooking in the world is vegan cooking - it can be truly horrible or it can be amazing. A well thought out meal includes a grain dish at its center; a well rounded range of root, round, green and/or sea veggies as well as well cooked beans or seeds. Pickles of some sort, soup or dessert complements these main dishes to bring out the lovely tastes and satisfaction. The overall effect isn't overly salty, spicy, sweet, dry nor wet. A fusion of foods from only one end of the expansive/contractive (yin /yang) continuum can be a bit gross and sometimes toxic.

Some examples are:

~ Cooking four or more different beans/seeds/nuts at once can be a dizzying overload of proteins. To find balance, simplify ones protein dishes and keep the bean and seeds at a minimum in any one meal.

~ Too many oily dishes... To find balance, add a fresh, pungent condiment (such as grated ginger or daikon radish with shoyu, slivered scallions, or kimchee) to cut through the oil.

~ Sweet soy desserts are pretty hard to balance: Soybeans are quite fatty and expansive to begin with, and once you refine the beans into milks or tofu, they are even more cooling and loosening. Salt nicely balances soy products. Sweeteners do not.

~ A totally raw salad made up of too many fibrous vegetables (such as cauliflower, broccoli, beets, etc) which may be more digestible when blanched.

~ A dish of nightshade vegetables (potatoes, eggplant, tomatoes) cooked together without much salt or time.... This can be super acidic and cause inflammation! To find balance, add plenty of salt, garlic and lots of time simmering or baking. Also, these combinations of nightshades are best eaten less often.

~ Too many unrelated dishes in one meal, such as one finds in a potluck. The solution is to leave some dishes at the table untasted.

COOKING METHODS

"I've learned that people will forget what you said, people will forget what you did, but people will never forget how you made them feel."
~ Maya Angelou, poet

There are about ten basic cooking methods, plus raw. Each method is unique and needed. Each method is simple, and powerfully different from the other methods. Once the intention of the method is understood, then any whole ingredients which are on hand can be appropriately cooked into a dynamic dish that complements the meal. Learning the spirit and specifics of the cooking methods is powerful, because it gives the cook the ability to get out of the way to let the flavors and energies shine through.

For an opening and brightening effect which gives quick energy, I could blanche leafy greens. For a gathering and fortifying effect, I might bake parsnips. A soft millet boiled with round, sweet veggies will be relaxing and loosen up any tightness; whereas dryer, pressure cooked millet will bestow centeredness and vigor…. Pressed salad with some citrus added will offer fresh restorative energy… Root vegetable nishime (long steamed in their own juices) will be tremendously soothing and settling to our systems. And so on… This is how menu planning happens and this is how an adventurous cook starts to hone his or her intuition.

> An interesting exercise to better understand the energetic distinctions between cooking methods is called the carrot class, from my teacher Aveline Kushi:
>
> Using only carrots (plus appropriate seasonings),
> the cook prepares these ten dishes:
>
> - PRESSED CARROT SALAD
> - RAW CARROT STICKS
> - BLANCHED CARROT SLICES
> - CARROT KINPIRA (QUICK SAUTÉ)
> - STEAMED CARROT ROUNDS
> - CARROT NISHIME (LONG STEAMED, IN ITS OWN JUICES)
> - CREME OF CARROT SOUP
> - CHUNKY CARROT STEW, LONG SAUTÉED THEN PRESSURE COOKED
> - WHOLE BAKED CARROT LOGS
> - CARROT TEMPURA
>
> Now the cook tastes each dish, noticing the different energies and effects.

The ten cooking methods and the continuum of energies they give are:

DEEP FRYING:
RICHENING, STIMULATING

FERMENTED/PRESSED SALAD:
REFRESHING, RESTORATIVE

BAKING:
GATHERING
DRYING

BLANCHED:
BRIGHTENING
OPENING

PRESSURE COOKING:
CENTERING
STRENGTHENING

WARMING ▲ | COOLING ▼
CONTRACTIVE   EXPANSIVE

QUICK STEAM:
LIGHTENING
YET CALMING

LONG SAUTÉ:
NOURISHING
GROUNDED ENERGY

QUICK SAUTÉ:
ENLIVENING
UPWARD ENERGY

LONG STEAM (NISHIME):
SETTLING, SOOTHING

BOILING:
RELAXING, LOOSENING

A NOTE ABOUT SALT AND SPICES:
If everything on the table always tastes salty, or spicy, it is the sign of an overly zealous cook who doesn't trust the subtle flavors of simple food... This can be hazardous to our health and disposition. Grains and beans, greens and roots are at their best when cooked well to bring out their subtle flavors, then flavored and garnished lightly. It's always most effective to seduce the eaters into the realms of what whole, real food actually tastes like, rather than trying to gussy up or cover up the foods with strong, addictive seasonings.

BASICS OF THE TEN COOKING METHODS (PLUS RAW):

Raw:
(COOLING)

Eating some raw salad or raw fruit can be quite cooling, perfect for a hot summer day, lightening and opening. A slice of watermelon or bowl of fresh tender lettuces from the garden are irreplaceable pleasures. Especially in the hot weather or to balance spicy, oily or animal foods, raw can add just the right touch to one's weekly menu. If overdone, especially for vegans, it can be weakening to the inner organs and, ultimately, unsatisfying. (Horses and cows have several stomachs to digest raw greens - but we do not.) Regularly drinking big store-bought bottles of juice is a common way to overdo RAW... Think about it - how many apples or carrots went into that bottle? (many pounds!)

Raw nuts and seeds are not very digestible and can introduce parasites, so these should always be toasted or boiled.

Basics for Raw Food:

• Eat fruits and salad greens in season, locally grown, whenever possible. Picking local wild fruits is one of the best adventures in children's lives - whether it be wild berries, crabapples or rosehips. Garden greens are bursting with juice and so delicately sweet that one hardly needs a dressing. Fresh garden carrots, turnips and cucumbers make a great snack, especially for the kids when they pick it themselves.

• An effective way to get a strong hit of RAW is to juice right in the kitchen. I like carrots with cabbage, kale or parsley. This juice is very concentrated, so a tiny portion goes a long way. It is a such relaxing remedy for overly tight conditions.

• Eat raw salad with a variety of dressings. Homemade dressings are easy to whip up. The best dressings include something of these tastes/qualities:

~ Oily or creamy (olive or sesame oil, tahini, tofu)

~ Salty (shoyu, salt, umeboshi, yellow miso)

~ Sweet (brown rice syrup, sautéed onions, sweet miso, grated carrots or apples, oranges)

~ Sour (vinegar, lemon, lime, umeboshi)

~ Pungent OR Bitter (garlic, scallion, onion, ginger, parsley, mustard)

FERMENTED:
(REFRESHING, RESTORATIVE)

Pickled vegetables, as well as pressed salads, are an essential important part of any well rounded grain-based diet. They feed beneficial micro-organisms which are essential for superior digestion. Pickling uses time, pressure and salt, rather than heat, as a form of cooking which transforms our raw ingredients and therefore pickles are a much more acceptable form of salty taste at the table (rather than raw salt).

I adore all sorts of pickled vegetables! Fermented foods are endlessly wonderful - kimchee, vinegars, sauerkraut, shoyu brines filled with garden radishes and greens, sinewy daikons pickled in bran, sour cucumbers, dilly beans, sweet relishes, bright pink radishes pressed with lemon rind and salt... the list is long and illustrious. Pickled vegetables lift the experience of a meal from merely humdrum to remarkable. Pickling and pressed salads come in many shapes and sizes, but here are some simple versions. The variations are endless.

THE PICKLE CROCK

To start an ongoing pickle crock, combine one part shoyu with two-three parts water. Now slice up some veggies thinly - onions, turnips and rutabaga and their greens, radish and daikon and their greens, napa cabbage and regular head cabbage, carrots, ginger, are all good. Layer them up in a clean glass jar or small crock. Pack the vegetables tightly. Pour the brine to cover completely. Cover the jar with a piece of cotton cheesecloth, or lay a leaf on top of the brine. Place on the counter and let ferment all week. It will bubble and gurgle. Once the vegetables taste sour, serve a few at each meal. If mold develops at the top of the jar, don't panic, it is perfectly safe. Simply scrape the mold off and discard. The vegetables deeply submerged in the brine will not mold. When the jar is empty, slice up some more vegetables to immerse in the brine. You can keep re-using the brine as long as it smells good - each time you refill, simply add a few more squirts of shoyu. Eventually, it will get kind of slimy. When that happens, discard the brine and start over fresh.

A variation of this is to start with one part shoyu, one part brown rice vinegar and one part water. This is especially delicious with rutabagas.

THE PICKLE CROCK #2

A salt brine with dill, garlic and coriander are wonderful for summery flavor. Use unrefined sea salt, about three tablespoons per quart of water, and proceed as above. Good vegetables for this are pickling cucumbers (used whole), green beans, napa cabbage, onions, cauliflower.

THE PICKLE CROCK #3

Refreshing, delicious and prettily pink pickles are made in a brine of one part ume vinegar to two parts water and sliced ginger . (The ginger is for flavoring the brine, not for eating). The best vegetables for this brine are daikon, radishes, white turnips, purple onions, cabbage and napa cabbage - all sliced thinly.

KRAUTS AND KIMCHEES

A longer term pickle we love is sauerkraut. We make it in a straight sided crock or bucket. Slice the cabbage thinly, add five tablespoons salt for every ten pounds shredded cabbage. It should look like a sprinkling of snow. Massage in the salt until the cabbage "weeps". Clean your crock meticulously, then sprinkle the sides with a bit of salt. Pack the cabbage inside tightly, pressing down and kneading with your clean hands to squeeze out any remaining air. Cover the crock with a plate and heavy weight (a stone or jar filled with water works best.) Then, cover the entire crock with a clean cloth, place in a cool yet not cold place, and wait. After 24 hours the juice should rise above the cabbage. If the water does not rise, then open it up and massage in some more salt. Once the cabbage is submerged under it's own juices, it is safe from molds. After three weeks, the sauerkraut will be ready to serve with meals. The crock will keep well in a cold place for many weeks if it lasts that long (because everyone always loves loves a good kraut!)

Simple kimchees can be made in the exact same manner, using any vegetables you like and adding garlic, red peppers, and/or ginger. My favorite is napa cabbage, with radishes and wild cucumber shoots.

LONG-TERM PICKLES

Miso and shoyu are my family's central long term fermented foods. They are vital for digesting grains and beans. The umeboshi plum itself is also a good long term pickle. We eat it with brown rice or add it to rice balls or nori rolls. We are beginning to make our own incredibly delicious miso, umeboshi and shoyu now, however the process is nuanced and description long so you will need further study to make these at home. Miso, shoyu and umeboshi can most economically be purchased wholesale through online macrobiotic food distributors*.

PRESSED SALAD

Pressed salad is a very refreshing side dish and adds freshness, crunch and zing to meals all year. The key to making refreshing pressed salad is to slice the vegetables very very thinly and use as little salt as possible by massaging the vegetables thoroughly. Cutting thinly takes a good sharp knife, big cutting board and practice.

My daughter Katie is a talented meticulous cook. When making pressed salads she takes her time and slices the vegetables thinner than I have ever seen, like delicate strands of hair. When I am cutting next to her we laugh, because she makes me look so bad. Everyone always flocks to eat her pressed salads, so juicy and flavorful.

These are the best vegetables for pressed salad: green cabbage, napa cabbage, radishes, daikon, carrots, cucumbers, lettuce, turnips, bokchoy, celery - also sometimes pears, apples, oranges or wakame seaweed.

After slicing thinly, mix the shredded vegetables in a big bowl and sprinkle with salt. It should look like a meadow barely dusted with snow. With clean hands, deliberately massage the salt into the vegetables until they start to "weep". For cucumbers, this happens quickly. For cabbage, it takes some time.

If the vegetables don't release lots of juice, add a bit more salt. Once the vegetables feel limp and quite juicy, then press with a heavy weight for one to three hours. A straight sided bowl or crock works best: gather the veggies into a pile, place a small plate on top, and then a river rock, or jar full of water, as a weight. The plate must not touch the sides of the bowl. Juice should then rise to cover the vegetables.

The salad is done when it no longer tastes "raw" - ideally, it should not taste salty either. If it is too salty, you can rinse it off but you will lose some of the vitamins and beneficial microbes. Discard some of the excess juice.

I like it best served with a light dressing, such as:

- grated carrot, grated green apple and lemon juice

- mashed tofu, olive oil and brown rice vinegar

- tahini and lemon juice

*see distributor list on page 50

Blanched:
(Opening, Brightening)

Blanched vegetables make a wonderful salad and satisfy ones' desire for crunch. One of my teachers, Denny Waxman, says that blanched should never be mushy and one should be able to hear the crunch of biting into a blanched salad from the other side of the room! Greens of all kinds (kale, collards, napa, mustard, turnip, radish, arugula, all the oriental greens, watercress, parsley), and roots (carrots, rutabagas, turnips, daikon and radishes) as well as celery, leeks, cauliflower, cabbage, broccoli, summer squashes and fresh peas, green beans and corn are all wonderful, and bring a bright gorgeous color to the table. We eat blanched salads five-ten times a week! They keep us flexible, light, open and young.

Blanching works best in a stainless pot, not too shallow nor too deep. I use a broad slotted spoon or handheld wire strainer to lift the veggies up out of the boiling water. A tray, or platter, on which to spread out the freshly blanched vegetables helps to keep the all important crunch.

Basics for Blanching:

• A pinch of salt in the boiling water will help keep the nutrients in the vegetables.

• Cut the vegetables thinly, so that they can cook thoroughly, yet stay crispy.

• Do not pour cold water over blanched vegetables to cool them off. Much of the light energy, vitamins and taste is lost that way. Instead, blanche quickly and spread out the steaming hot veggies on a platter or tray to cool, before tossing them together in a serving bowl. This way, the salad won't overcook in the bowl.

• Eat blanched salads plain sometimes, and other times with a light dressing or a sprinkle of vinegar or lemon. A wonderful, simple dressing is olive oil and ume vinegar.

• Different vegetables can be mixed together for an eye-pleasing and varied salad. Mix light greens with dark greens or mix and match bright colors: for white - daikon, turnips, cauliflower; for orange/yellow - carrots, rutabaga, leeks, corn, summer squash; for red and purple - radishes, purple cabbage or beets.

Quick Sauté:
(enlivening, upward energy)

Quickly sautéed veggies are made famous by oriental "stir fry". I enjoy them with a variety of vegetables but also with only one. The energy of this dish is rousing and boosting yet a bit richer and punchier than blanching. I like to sauté up some bitter greens like mustards, dandelions or arugula with a little bit of shoyu and mirin (sweet vinegar). A quick sauté is a good pair with pasta or other whole grain product such as couscous. It cheers up a rainy day.

My preferred pots for sautéing are stainless or cast iron - wide and more shallow with two sturdy handles. It always comes out tastier if I match the size of the pot with the amounts of vegetables that I am wanting to sauté.

Basics for Quick Sauté:

- Use sesame, sunflower or olive oil, and add the vegetables quickly so that the oil doesn't burn in the pan. Alternatively, use a little bit of water only, at first, then add a dash of oil just before the dish is done. This makes for an even lighter sauté.

- Slice the vegetables nice and thin so that they cook up crispy quickly.

- Season with a bit of salt, shoyu or ume vinegar toward the end of cooking to bring out the sweetness of the vegetables.

Kinpira

One of my favorite dishes is a quick sauté made from strong root vegetables.

Use one, two or three of these root vegetables: carrots, burdock, rutabaga, turnip, onion, parsnip, daikon, lotus root. My favorite combination is carrots, burdock and lotus root; also just parsnips.

1) Cut the roots into thinnest matchsticks.

2) Heat up a pan, coat the bottom with sesame oil, then add the match-sticked root vegetables one kind at a time. Add the most dense first for a few minutes, then the softer ones (burdock first, then lotus root, then carrots, for example).

3) Stir the roots constantly over a high heat, adding a sprinkling of salt to bring out the juices of the vegetables. Kinpira takes a bit longer than usual quick sautés because these root vegetables are dense and firm. Sometimes, you need to add a bit of water while you stir.

4) When the veggies are cooked yet still a bit crispy, add a dash of shoyu and a smidgen of grated ginger juice.

This dish has a dynamic fiery energy, sweet and salty taste, and is a big favorite in the winter time.

Quick Steam:
(Lightening yet calming)

Steaming vegetables is more settling than blanching or sautéing, and so I try to use it regularly also, for variety. Steaming brings a steady light energy to round and root vegetables and brings out the minerals in greens.

I have explored many nice steamers: from the flower, fold up variety, to the stacking bamboo steamers which are sold in Asian shops, to the colander type stainless steamer which nests inside its own pot. I especially like the large rectangular restaurant steamers, because I often cook for many people. It is easier to effectively steam with a lot of space inside the steamer. These are inexpensive and handy for large families.

Basics for Quick Steaming Vegetables:

• Steam large amounts of veggies in smaller batches, so that they cook evenly.

• Try to refrain from peeking while steaming - every time the top comes off, all the gathered steam is lost.

• Unlike blanching, steamed vegetables stop cooking as soon as they come off of the heat. Therefore, make sure that the greens are cooked through and through before pulling them out of the steamer.

• I eat steamed greens plain some of the time, and with a dressing some of the time. A super dressing is olive oil and umeboshi vinegar.

BOILING:
(RELAXING, LOOSENING)

Boiling grains and beans is a little lighter, and more relaxing, than pressure cooking. Grain or bean soups and stews, vegetable broths, vegetable miso soups and creamy chowders are a daily need, and a relaxing way to assimilate food. Learning to make luscious soup is a necessity for successful cooking without recipes.

One of my all time best soups is winter squash, boiled then blended, with a bit of salt and ginger added at the end - simple, and so great.

My best boiling pots are stainless or enameled, and have a heavier bottom and a well fitting lid.

BASICS FOR BOILING GRAINS:

• Soak brown rice, barley and whole oats to make them more digestible. Measure the grain with the water, and then soak for six - twelve hours. No need to soak millet, quinoa, or buckwheat, as these grains soften quickly. For a nice chewable brown rice, soak, then boil one and a half cups of water per cup of rice.

• A pinch of salt per cup of grain is a good baseline salt amount.

• To make fluffy sweet millet, buckwheat, or quinoa, first dry roast the grains in a skillet until golden and aromatic. Then, dice some round vegetables such as onions, carrots, cabbage, winter squash. Then, layer up the diced vegetables in a pot, and combine with one part toasted grain and three parts water. Add a few pinches of salt, bring to a boil and simmer on a heat diffusing pad for thirty minutes.

• For a grain porridge, boil one part of any grain with four parts water (except barley which needs six parts water). In a separate pot, simmer round and root vegetables until sweet. Then, add both pots together, and simmer until creamy. Season with miso, and/or shoyu, and grated ginger or other herbs, such as cilantro, if you like.

Basics for Boiling Beans:

• Soak most beans for at least six hours. Discard the soaking water and add fresh before cooking, to prevent gassiness.

• Add a three inch piece of kombu or bay leaf to help soften beans. Add seasonings toward the end of cooking, rather than the start. Beans combine well with onions - lots of onions.

• For boiled bean stews: soak beans with water to cover for six hours. Discard the beans' soaking water, bring to a boil with fresh water, a piece of kombu (kelp), and simmer until soft (sometimes many hours). In a separate pot, layer up round and root vegetables with some water to cover and bubble on their own until sweet. Combine together, to make a hardy soup or stew. Season with fresh greens like parsley or cilantro as well as shoyu or miso, and perhaps a dash of olive oil.

Basics for Boiling Broths/Soups:

• For miso or shoyu broths, simmer any round or root vegetables until soft and sweet. Add dried mushrooms, if you like. At the end of cooking, add some bright greens and/or sea vegetables (for example wakame, or kale). Then season with miso, or shoyu, to taste. Garnish with minced scallions, parsley or cilantro.

My favorite combinations are:
~ onion, daikon, shiitake mushrooms and wakame (sea vegetable) miso soup
~ leek, squash, carrots, corn, kale miso soup
~ "kinpira soup": Sauté matchsticks of carrots, lotus root, burdock, and cubes of winter squash, then boil until very sweet. This is best seasoned with a combination of sweet white miso and barley miso.
~ chunky onions, carrots, cabbage, kombu (sea vegetable) and dried shiitake mushrooms in a shoyu broth

• For creamy vegetable soups, boil onions with cauliflower, broccoli, winter squash, carrots, or other sweet root vegetables. Add more than a few pinches of salt while cooking. Blend until creamy and serve with a yummy garnish such as sautéed leeks, parsley or crunchy deep-fried croutons.

Long Steam (Nishime):
(settling, soothing)

Nishime is a soothing, centering, calming dish made from root and round vegetables cooked for a long time primarily in their own juices. Nishime brings out the exquisitely sweet flavors of each vegetable. I've learned that nishime supports the middle organs (stomach, spleen, pancreas) and is very good for diabetes prevention and treatment. Making nishime well is an art worth learning. We eat nishime three or four times a week to keep grounded.

Use a pot with a tight fitting heavy lid (enameled cast iron pots are perfect, but a stainless pot with a good lid works well too. I place two hand-size stones on top of a stainless lid, transforming it into a heavier lid.) Ideally, the pot should be the right size to be filled just to the brim with the chunky vegetables.

Also, long steamed bread is a lovely alternative to baked bread. Fluffy, moist and delicious, this is highly digestible whole grain bread, perfect for people, like me, who get inordinately wiped out by dry, baked flour products.

For how to make steamed bread, see page 32.

Nishime

1) Cut the vegetables very big and chunky. Carrots, onions, winter squash, daikon radish, rutabaga, turnips, burdock and leeks all make good nishime.

2) Place a three inch piece of kombu plus a tiny bit of water in the bottom of the pot. The water should barely cover the entire bottom of the pot. If there is too much water, the finished dish will lack vitality and sweetness.

3) Layer the vegetables in the pot. First, spread the juicier, rounder and/or softer vegetables in the bottom of the pot, then layer the drier, harder vegetables on top.

4) Cover, bring to a high steam and immediately turn the flame down to a very low simmer. Resist the urge to lift the lid, and peek at the vegetables, as they will lose plenty of liquid each time one opens the lid. If the fire is too high, it is easy to burn, so the flame needs to be just high enough for the steaming to continue.

5) Cook slowly, until completely soft and sweet, perhaps fifty minutes. The juices of the vegetables will come out as they steam. If one started with just a smidgen of extra water, one will get the sweetest, most comforting dish ever, with just a bit of condensed juice in the bottom of the pot.

LONG SAUTÉ:
(NOURISHING, GROUNDING)

Hardy, warming and delicious, long time sauté is a wonderful way to coax the sweetness from root and round vegetables. Onion butter, squash puree, sweet sautéed parsnips, rutabaga and burdock are all winter favorites, quite satisfying and strengthening.

My favored pots for a long sautéed dish are cast iron dutch ovens. Stainless steel is also serviceable if it has a heavy bottom, and heavy lid.

BASICS FOR LONG SAUTÉ:

• Use plenty of sesame oil, either light or toasted, for best flavor and strengthening energy, and add a pinch of salt to bring out the juices of the vegetables.

• Add a minimum of water as the vegetables cook. Juicier veggies, like onions, don't need any water at all.

• Cover and simmer/sauté with a low heat for a long time, stirring regularly to prevent scorching, and season to taste with salt or shoyu.

Pressure Cooking:
(strengthening, centering)

Pressure cooking is good for strong, centered, scrumptious grains and beans. (Vegetables rarely need pressure-cooking.) I use pressure-cooking every day. My good friend, Mayumi Nishimura, once gave a televised cooking class in Japan, in which she pressure-cooked a simple pot of brown rice, and that's all. It was inspiring because it was so basic, yet nuanced.

Pressure-cooked short grain brown rice is exceptionally strengthening, and kind of miraculous. It is an art worth getting just right. When well chewed, it is a deeply satisfying center for one's weekly menu. We make it five - ten times per week for sustainable vitality. We regularly add other grains, seeds, or beans to rice to make varied dishes with subtle distinctions: millet-rice, barley-rice, wheat-rice, kidney-bean-rice, aduki-bean-rice, chestnut-rice, rice with walnuts or pumpkin seeds. We also make long grain rice and sweet (sticky) rice for an endless array of meals.

There are a few good pressure cookers on the market now. I like Kuhn Rikon Duromatics, as well as Silit Sicomatics. Always use stainless or enamel - never aluminum. I also use a "flame tamer" or heat diffusing pad, once it comes up to pressure to keep the heat low and even. This prevents the grain or beans from forming a sticky crust, or worse, burning.

Basics for Pressure Cooking Grains:

• Generally speaking, pressure cooking needs a 1/4 less water and a 1/4 less time than boiling the same dish. How much water to add depends on the desired consistency: generally, two to one is dry and fluffy, five to one is porridgy. Experiment to see what works for you.

• Soak the harder grains - brown rice, barley, oat groats or wheat berries - for at least six hours before pressure cooking. (For wheat, soak for 24 hours.)

• For brown rice, one and one third cups of water to each cup of short grain rice makes a fine, chewable dish that will give plenty of energy. Don't forget to add a pinch of salt for each cup of rice. Pressure cook for forty minutes. When it is done and down from pressure, use a wooden paddle to stir the rice from top to bottom in a spirally motion, adding air and fluffing up the rice. Serve in a wooden or ceramic bowl. This makes the sweetest, most delicious and attractive brown rice ever.

• Millet only needs twenty minutes of pressure-cooking, whereas wheat, oats or barley want almost sixty. (For instructions on cooking grain corn, see page 33.) When the pressure-cooking time is over, let the pot cool down. Once it is down from pressure, open the pot and stir up the contents. If you are in a hurry, you can tug on the pressure gauge to let the steam out.

Basics for Pressure Cooking Beans:

• Most beans need to be soaked overnight in order to soften up properly. The exceptions are: split peas, red lentils, black eyed peas. Discard the soaking water and add fresh before cooking, to prevent gassiness.

• For dryer bean dishes, add two parts water for each part beans. For softer stews, add three parts of water for each part beans.

• Use a piece of kombu (kelp) or bay leaf, to soften up the beans. Add salt towards the end of cooking, rather than at the start.

• Most beans need an hour of pressure cooking - the exceptions are lentils, split peas and black eyed peas, which only need twenty minutes.

Baking:
(gathering, drying)

Baked dishes are somehow more cheery than other dishes. Baking aromas often make my mouth water! Baking can be very warming and fortifying, good for cold winter days. Overdone, too much baked foods can lead to an overly dry and tight condition but in the colder weather it can be quite satisfying. We love baked vegetables, polenta casseroles, and baked lima beans with onions and mustard at my house. Sweet, rich Alaska grown parsnips, or winter squash, baked in a deep dish with olive oil and salt consistently gets lots of smiles.

Baking dishes are very individual. Clay or enamel is nice, but quite breakable and they don't last long in my life. Glass is a good alternative. If the baking dish doesn't have a lid, one will often need to use another dish or aluminum foil as a cover.

Basics for Baking:

- For baked vegetables, oil and salt the veggies then add a smidgen of water in the bottom of the baking dish, and cover well so that they don't get too dry.

- For baking beans, soak and pre-boil the beans first in lots of water. Then, discard the excess water, add plenty of sautéed, sweet veggies, and seasonings (miso, shoyu, olive oil, rice syrup or barley malt, mustard). Bake all together for many hours on low heat.

- Before baking pears or apples, you can scoop out the core and fill with tahini/almond butter/raisins/rice syrup/cinnamon/vanilla.

- Baked treats made with flour - pies, cakes, cookies, crackers, crumbles, and crunches - are quite drying, and hard on our digestion and will. "Weak digestion, weak mind." Remember that the stomach tries to make all food into soup to prepare it for its journey down the intestines. Imagine how much liquid it has to pull in for a bowl of crackers. Eat these kinds of desserts once in awhile just to prove that one can be as decadent as one wants. It is helpful to learn to make them with whole vegan ingredients and mild sweeteners. There are many great cookbooks that feature amazing natural desserts on the market.

Baked Mochi Muffins

1) Preheat oven to 400 degrees. Spoon mochi dough onto an oiled cookie sheet.

2) Bake for 20 minutes, or until puffed up into little mochi "muffins."

3) Eat these hot, with blanched vegetable salad and a sesame tahini sauce.

Blend tahini with a bit of water and miso or shoyu. This simple sauce is tasty and nutritious. Toddlers love it and it is good for their bone growth.

Deep Frying:
(Richening, Stimulating)

Deep fried foods have a fiery, stimulating energy, and are simultaneously incredibly rich, warming and nurturing. Deep frying is everybody's favorite and can be easily overdone, but once or twice a week for most people in good health, it is quite satisfying. My favorite is deep fried aduki-rice balls: OH MY. Always serve deep fried foods with a balancing pungent condiment of ginger/shoyu/scallions, grated daikon mixed with shoyu, mustard, or horseradish, to cut the excess oiliness.

A cast iron dutch oven, or a wok, makes an ideal deep frying pot. Also needed is a wire mesh, hand-held strainer for pulling out the finished product from the hot oil; and a good spot to drain and cool.

Deep Fried Aduki Bean Rice Balls

1) Soak three cups short grain brown rice and one cup aduki beans together overnight with six cups of water.

2) In the morning, pressure cook, with three pinches of salt, for 45 minutes. Cool and let pressure naturally come down.

3) Spread out aduki rice on a platter to cool. Fill a small bowl with water. Wet your hands and grab a large handful of cooked bean-rice. Using both hands, press the rice firmly to create a ball, like a small snow ball. Keep turning and pressing the ball of bean-rice until it is very firm. The rice-ball can be round, or triangular, or shaped like a burger patty. Place the rice balls in rows on a tray.

4) Deep fry until crispy and serve hot with grated daikon radish and shoyu or grated ginger/shoyu.

Basics for Deep Frying:

• Use sunflower or safflower oil. Other oils will burn, or foam up into a huge mess.

• To identify the perfect temperature: drop a piece of food into the oil. If it sinks to the bottom and stays there, the oil is too cold. If it jumps at the top of the oil, the oil is too hot. Ideally, the piece of food drops briefly downward, then bobs to the top, sizzling quietly.

• To make deep fried rice balls, cook the rice freshly and, while hot, form the balls with your hands, using water to prevent sticking.

• Other grain patties, such as millet and barley, are also great - but you must cook the grains with enough water (and sweet vegetables if you like) so that they aren't at all crumbly! My favorite is millet cooked with onions, squash and carrots.

• To deep fry vegetables (tempura), make a thin batter with beer or bubbly water, pastry and/or oat flour and pinch of salt. Slice up your veggies, thinly. Dip the vegetables in the batter, then deep fry each piece until golden brown. Let the tempura cool down on a rack, or paper towels, to drain the oil before serving.

• When finished, cover the pot, cool down in a safe spot, strain the oil and keep in a cool, dark place. A glass jar works well for storage. The oil can be reused four or five times (as long as it hasn't been burned).

DELICIOUS DESSERTS:

"If you want to make an apple pie from scratch, you must first create the universe." ~ Carl Sagan

Cooking desserts has never been my forte. I have burned more nuts and ruined more pie dough than most have probably attempted. Once in awhile, I haul out the dessert cookbooks and follow a recipe… and produce a legendary elaborate cake or parfait. But I am happier with simpler sweets, and with my live ingredients in front of me, talking to me directly about how they want to be prepared. Breezy kantens or rich fruit compotes are all I really need to make for a happy evening.

Kids love every kind of sweet, and have an uncanny radar that can find the apples, or honey, or candies in any house. Figuring out how to make edible sweets for the kids is a mother's pleasure. Except for the occasional melon on a hot summer day, it's preferable to cook fruit for children, because it becomes less acidic.

Often at my house, the kids will be eating sourdough muffins with raisins, or oatmeal-walnut cookies with brown rice syrup, or home-made amasake drink. Amasake is a fermented rice milkshake easily made at home with store-bought rice koji/starter. (When you purchase the koji, it comes with detailed instructions.) The kids can help make it, they love it, and it's so good for them!

An all-time best-loved treat in the winters is apple or berry pie. A refreshing spring and summer dessert which everyone loves is fruit kanten, a natural light "jello" or pudding. I top both pies and kantens with some mint leaves, or sweet whipped nut creme and fresh berries.

My kids also love to cook up rice syrup candies. I used to hide plenty of these wrapped nut candies around the house for a big, fun, treasure hunt. Then months later, I would find the odd candy in my sock drawer, where it had been forgotten.

---

3 Versions of Sweet Cremes

- **To make sweet creme from nuts:** boil almonds or pecans for twenty minutes. Drain but save the cooking water. If using almonds, peel them by squeezing each nut between your fingers. The peels will easily slip away. Puree the nuts in a blender with vanilla and maple or brown rice syrup, and a bit of cooking water if necessary, until smooth and creamy.

- **To make sweet creme from tofu:** puree fresh, raw tofu with vanilla and maple or brown rice syrup to taste in a blender until creamy.

- **To make sweet creme from oat, almond or rice milk:** Combine two cups of the milk with two tablespoons agar agar (gelatinous sea vegetable) flakes and soak for ten minutes. Add maple or rice syrup, as well as vanilla, to taste. Bring to a boil and simmer for ten minutes. Pour into a deep baking dish, and place in a cold spot for an hour or more, until it sets up. Once it is firm, blend well until creamy.

Fruit Pie

1) CRUST: The basic crust is one cup pastry flour, one cup white flour, big pinch of salt, half cup sunflower oil and half cup water or soy milk. Mix the flours and salt; mix the water (or soy milk) and oil; briefly whisk the wet and dry ingredients together for a manageable, flaky dough.

2) FILLING: Slice up the raw fruit, or sort through the berries. Powder a little bit of kuzu by grinding it in a blender or suribachi (mortar and pestle). Sprinkle the kuzu powder over the fruit, along with a few pinches of salt. It should resemble a light snow. Drizzle brown rice syrup or maple syrup over the fruit, and a splash of vanilla. (Amounts will depend on many factors - taste the fruit and use your intuition.) Mix well.

3) Place the fruit filling into the pie crust, add a top crust, flute the edges, and bake it all together in a 350 degree oven until golden (about 40 minutes). Cool before serving with a sweet creme topping.

Rice Syrup Candies

1) In a dry pan, separately toast sesame seeds, pecans, almonds, walnuts and/ or sunflower seeds until golden and smelling sweet.

2) Combine two cups of brown rice syrup with a dash of light oil in a pot, over a medium flame. Stir constantly as it begins to simmer.

3) Lower the flame, stirring for ten - twenty minutes, until the color darkens into a caramel brown. Keep checking the mixture by dripping it onto a cool plate. Once the drops harden as they cool, the syrup is finished cooking.

4) Mix the seeds and/or nuts into the cooling syrup. Pour out the mixture onto a plate or tray to cool.

5) When it is just cool enough to handle, roll pieces into little round candies to harden. When completely cool, wrap each candy individually in a small square of baking paper.

Fruit Kanten

1) Soak agar-agar (gelatinous sea vegetable) flakes in fruit juice for ten minutes: one tablespoon agar per cup of juice.

2) Bring to a boil, stir, and simmer for ten minutes.

3) While the juice is simmering, cut up some fresh soft fruits (berries, melons, and peaches are the best) into bite size chunks. Fill the bottom of a deep baking dish or jello mold with the raw fruit.

4) Pour the steaming juice over the fresh fruit, and place in a cold spot for an hour or more, until it sets.

Another version of this frothy dessert is to blend it until creamy, at the end. This makes a smooth creme which you can serve with sweet cookies, toasted nuts or fresh berries.

Fruit Compote

1) Stew up apples, pears, peaches or berries with a bit of water and pinch of salt.

2) If needed, add a dollop of brown rice syrup for more sweetness.

3) Dissolve some kuzu (root starch) in a cup of cold water. Stir it into the bubbling, simmering fruit to thicken up the juices. This make the dish more like a fruit pudding, and wonderfully digestible.

4) Top with toasted pecans or walnuts.

NOURISHMENT ON THE ROAD

"Not all those who wander are lost." ~ *J.R.R. Tolkien, novelist*

My mother is fond of pointing out that if you go to town without packing lunch, you will eat out. And, no doubt, there will usually be concentrated foods involved. Sometimes, of course, that's a perk. However, if that becomes more of a punishment, necessarily you become like a camel in the desert, carrying your life source. In order to eat actual meals (not that packaged stuff) while running around town, at work or at school, you can pack an emergency food kit: toasted sesame seeds or almonds; raw scallions or kale, and nori or dulse (sea vegetables) crumbled up, ready for instant soup; miso and shoyu in small travel size containers; and some sauerkraut or other vegetable pickles. Add to that your grain of the day.

Soup in a thermos, of course is wonderful. A pressed salad always hits the spot. Rice-balls and nori rolls are some of our favorite ways to bring whole grain with us on the road. If we are traveling long distances for many days, we have discovered home-canning as a handy solution for keeping cooked food fresh. It is great to know that you have food with you, wherever you go, and that you won't be stranded in the middle of a mall sorrowfully consuming yet another sorry salad and unfortunate baked potato while staring despondently at the fast-food joint menus.

EVERY DAY RICE BALLS

cooked brown rice (cooked with 1 1/2 parts water to 1 part rice for a sticky/chewy consistency)
umeboshi paste or plum
sheet of toasted nori (sea vegetable)
optional: almond butter or tahini

1) Fill a small bowl with water. Wet your hands and grab a large handful of cooked rice. Using both hands, press the rice firmly to create a ball, like a snow ball. Keep turning and pressing the ball of rice until it is very firm. The rice-ball can be round, or triangular, or shaped like a burger patty.

2) On top, spread a a dab of umeboshi paste or plum, and if you like, a dollop of almond butter or tahini.

3) Cut the sheet of nori in 4 pieces. Carefully wrap one piece around the ball of rice. Repeat with one more square, so that the rice is mostly covered with nori.

4) Wrap the rice-ball in wax paper or brown paper. Throw it in your pocket or purse, and you are good to go.

Nori rolls

cooked brown rice (cooked with 1 1/2 parts water to 1 part rice for a sticky/chewy consistency)
toasted sesame seeds OR tahini
umeboshi paste or plum OR sauerkraut
steamed carrot matchsticks
raw scallions, minced
sheet of toasted nori (sea vegetable)
optional: tofu, or tempeh, cut into strips and fried

1) Lay out all of your ingredients on the counter, as well as a bowl of water.

2) Lay a sheet of nori flat on the counter. Wet your hands and spread a handful of brown rice onto the bottom half of the nori sheet.

3) On the lower edge, spread a thin line of tahini or toasted sesame seeds, plus umeboshi or sauerkraut. Add matchsticks of carrots as well as some fried tofu or tempeh strips, if you have them. There should be an even line of ingredients from left to right. Sprinkle on raw, minced scallions.

4) Holding all the ingredients tightly in place with your fingers, roll up the nori with the rice and vegetables inside, bottom to top, like a sleeping bag or towel. With your finger, wet the top edge of the sheet of nori, before finishing the roll. Squeeze the roll carefully, yet firmly, to seal it like an envelope.

5) With a sharp wet knife, cut the roll into quarters, then into eighths, for a pretty and delicious lunch.

We love these nori rolls dipped in a wasabi/shoyu sauce for a touch of spicy goodness!

Home-Canned Grains and Nishime

These jars of food are heavy and fragile, yet the amazing upside is that you will have safe, preserved real food for many days and even weeks. You can give each person their own, to carry in their travel bag. And, you can preserve baby porridge this way.

To cook and preserve grains:

1) In the evening, soak brown rice, millet, barley, or even buckwheat directly into pint or quart size
canning jars. For a pint size jar, soak 1/2 cup of rice in 3/4 cup of water. For millet or buckwheat, try 1/2 cup of grain to 1 1/4 cups of water, plus you can add a few diced onions or carrots.

2) In the morning, add a pinch of salt and close the jars tightly.

3) Place the jars in several inches of water. The water should not come over the top of the jar. Bring to a boil and simmer for 2 hours in a covered pot. Keep an eye out that the water doesn't boil away completely.

4) Cool the jars on the counter. As the jars cool, the lids will suck down to create a vacuum seal. (If the lid is not sealed, discard the jar of food.)

For fresh root vegetables:

1) Cut root vegetables in large chunks and layer up the chunks, filling a canning jar.

2) Add an inch of kombu (kelp) and pour 3 T of water over the roots.

3) and 4) as above.

chapter five

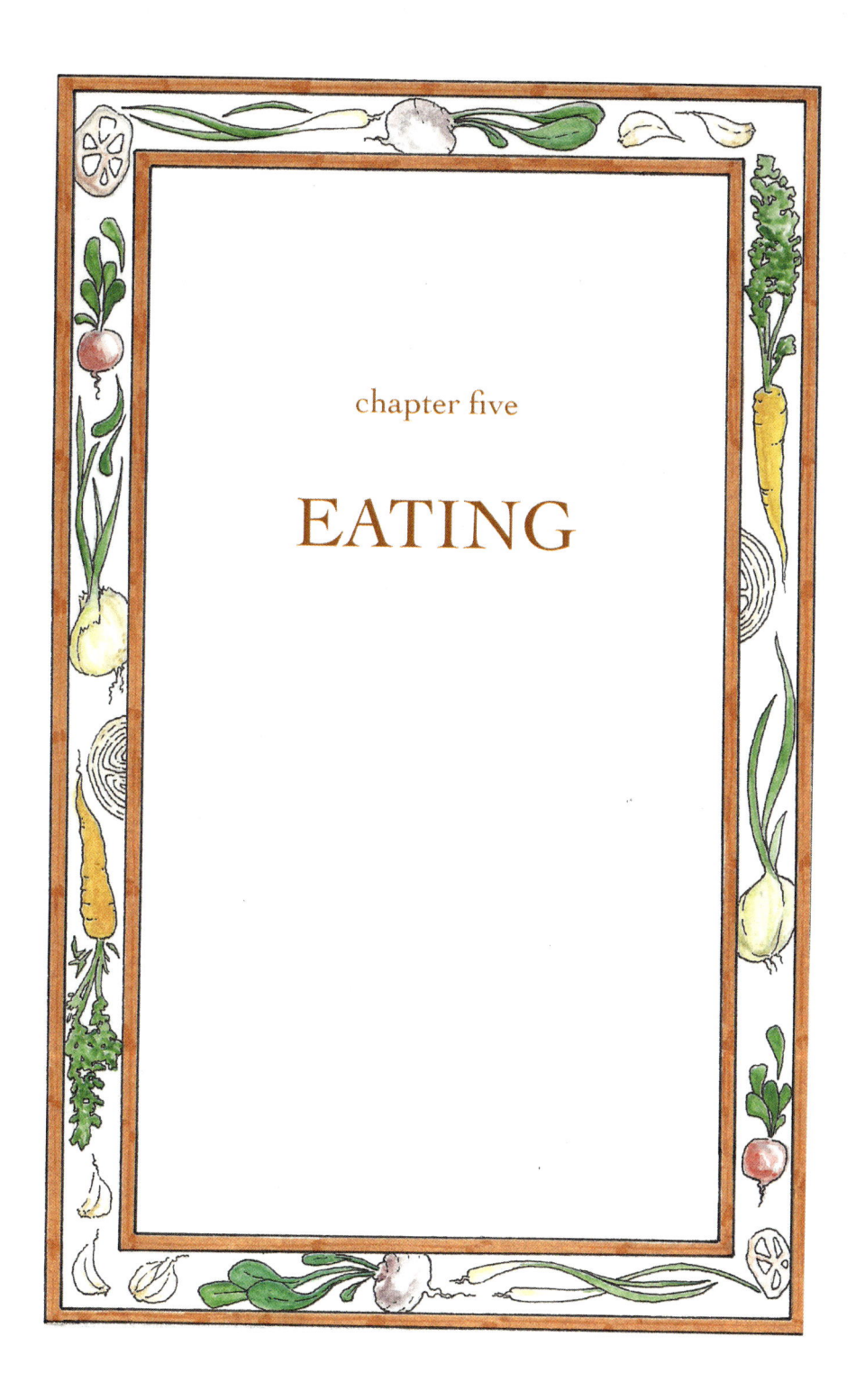

EATING

SWEETS AND ADDICTIONS

"My soul is dark with stormy riot,
 Directly traceable to diet."
 ~ *Samuel Hoffenstein, screenwriter and composer*

People are hard wired to love the sweet taste, beginning as infants with our mother's milk. Our body needs sugars. So, the factor to ponder over is, what is the source of the sugar? How has it been concentrated and refined from the original source? And, when I crave something very sweet, or strong, why is that?

Sweet taste is all a matter of comparison. When one's taste buds are quieted down, the milder sugars in whole grains and round vegetables become very satisfying. Chewing a bite of whole grain 100 x or more releases the complex sugars, creating a sweet ambrosia with a similar taste to mother's milk. Slow cooked sweet vegetables like onions, carrots, burdock, corn, winter squash, rutabagas, parsnips and cabbage satisfy those cravings for quieter sweet. Daily soups sweetened up with these intense vegetables are deeply nourishing.

To amp it up a bit if one desires a more potent sweet taste, there are un-refined grain sourced sweeteners such as brown rice syrup, barley malt and amasake*; as well as pure maple and birch syrups, genuine agave, dried fruits and unrefined fruit juices. Desserts made from these less condensed sweeteners can be eaten every week without creating much tempest in the bloodstream. "Simple sugars" in fruits hit our bloodstream very quickly - right through the tongue - whereas the more complex sugars in grains are processed through the intestines so they have an evener, slower effect. Experiment and see what leaves your body the calmest.

My understanding is that the most concentrated sugars available today are high fructose corn syrup and refined cane sugar. However, these have hundreds of commercial names. I experience molasses, honey and the artificial sweeteners (such as xylitol) as highly concentrated as well. These types of sweeteners burn hot, and create a powerful physical addiction with its own desires. I find that the more concentrated and refined the sugar, the more addictive. It is similar to alcohol, nicotine, caffeine and other drugs, in their abilities to speed life up, add some higher highs and lower lows to ones' emotional and energetic mix. Crack is not far behind.

Drugs are so magical, that they often bypass the body's hunger for real food. Sometimes, the familiarity of the addiction is more delicious than anything else, because it is part of our deepest memories… Familiar hits of concentration become woven into who we know ourselves to be. In my mind, the more surreptitious, cunning drugs are the every day stimulants of coffee, cigarettes, alcohol, candy and colas. These give us strong boosts of up and down energy to which we become addicted swiftly and noiselessly, with society's blessing. Most of us are infatuated at an early age to that fast hit of refined sugars. This can easily become fierce addiction to alcohol, medications or street drugs later in life. While most of us become enslaved to some sort of food at some point in our lifetime (sugar, alcohol, coffee, marijuana, bread, eggs, cheese, milk, cigarettes, salt, white flour) it usually serves an unconscious, or semi-conscious, purpose in our life. Charles Eisenstein, a wise modern thinker and author, says "Addiction, self-sabotage, procrastination, laziness, rage, chronic fatigue, and depression are all ways that we withhold our full participation in the program of life we are offered. When the conscious mind cannot find a reason to say no, the unconscious says no in its own way." To unwind and replace these habits can

*see page 81 for more about amasake

take real practical and interconnected steps down a hopeful path that speaks to us, beyond food or health, that we feel is possible and desirable.

To begin to unravel our drive for sugars, one begins by replacing baked flours, salty dry chips and crackers, baked breads, and animal foods with whole grains.... My process over the years about sweets has been long and not so illustrious. My unfortunate tendency to fall into hopeless black holes was linked to my penchant for over-indulging on simple sugars and it took me many moons to get this craziness under control. I mostly weaned myself off of corn syrup and white sugar very early on in life, when I started to get pregnant regularly; and these addictions were replaced with the afternoon hit of fruit sugars, maple syrup, rice syrup, even white pasta. My blood sugar starts to fall and, more often than not, I look for sweets, or white flour, to prop it up again… and my process zigzags forward in a huge spiral. I am slowly working my way up some twisted list of every sweet thing in the health food section. At some point, I am positive that I will be finally and irrevocably done with any store-bought sweets. I've learned that when I lower salt intake, and dry, baked floury foods, my sweet cravings subside. I've also noticed that my taste buds are very malleable, and that when I do direct my sails toward simpler fare, it takes a fairly short time (three days) to fall in love again with whole grains and sweet vegetables.

Some say that changing one's diet is harder and less likely than changing one's religion. Lifelong eating habits are ingrained. We eat what our parents taught us to eat; how our tastes developed as a young child; what our peers and society serve up; we eat according to our culture. Be that as it may, I have seen that our deepest appetite, it turns out, is in charge and more powerful even than lifelong habits or cultural norms... we must follow it according to our sensitivities, or we will truly be lost.

To step out of one's culture and surroundings in order to follow an inner food path requires giving up many rights and urges to "fit in," and be fed by one's extended family and community institutions. It is a courageous step, but also a deeply nourishing one. As someone once said, reality is for those who can't handle drugs. There is an extraordinary experience of calm there.

ENVIRONMENT OF EATING

"We inter-breath with the rain forests, we drink from the oceans. They are part of our own body."
~ Thich Nhat Hanh, monk, teacher and peace activist

The other half of cooking is how our food is eaten. Most everybody loves to eat. Eating is life affirming, it is one of the innate pleasures of being alive, and often, our warmest memories are linked to eating.

There are at least three big actors that I have noticed in the play of eating well:

Chewing
Time of day
Environment

Chewing

Once, I embarked on a silence fast wherein I deliberately stopped talking for three days altogether. My reasons were general unhappiness, overwhelming busyness, seeming inability to cope with my life stresses and find my center, my bigger life direction. So... I simply stopped talking. My responses and reactions floated by but I didn't voice them. My children soon bored of asking me questions and I watched the play of humanity around me from a distance.

The first thing that I noticed is my heightened awareness of my body's place in the world. Standing, sitting, walking, and eating became more pleasurable as my attention settled into the now. Chewing well became more possible.

Over the years, I have learned that chewing each bite of food until it is liquid is a magic wand to transform all that we eat into pure accessible energy. Chewing is more than just chomping and mashing - it is a meditation – a pathway to being present. One of my teachers, Denny Waxman, says that to improve health, simply chew each bite one hundred times; to maintain health, chew fifty times; and to lose health, chew less than that. Saliva is a prime digestive agent, full of active bacteria vital to the bodies ability to assimilate nutrients. As we chew more, we eat less, yet have more energy.

I like to ponder upon the wood stove analogy: If we don't chew well, it is much like burning wet firewood in a wood stove: sixty percent of the heat of the fire is going to be used to steam all the water out of the wood, and subsequently lost up the chimney. One must burn three times as much firewood to heat one's home, and all that extra firewood stresses one's wood splitter and pocketbook. Similarly, if one doesn't chew ones food much of the potential energy within the ingredients is burned up in extra processing. One will have to eat two to three times as much food to function well. All that extra food stresses one's system, and pocketbook.

Just as importantly, through chewing, I've noticed that my family's attitudes change from merely a critic and consumer, to co-creator and full participant in the experience of that meal. Someone takes responsibility for how they eat, and therefore, how they feel. This is quite powerful. Every year, as I learn to take time with meals more and more, I see chewing as an inconvenient truth, the personal food revolution.

Talking around the dinner table is a well-worn cultural custom, however it is very challenging (practically impossible) to chew one's meal while keeping up an active conversation. At Ionia, we sometimes practice the social custom of quiet meals. Eating while reading, eating at the computer, or eating while standing or walking are all discouraged. Eating is seen as the perfect opportunity NOT to multitask, nor check in with anyone excepting our own selves. Because chewing is both a social and private challenge I highly respect attempts to clear away the noisy hub-bub, busy-ness and social expectations in order to find a quiet haven to pay attention to one's meal. This is the cutting edge work of a new generation of "way of life" pioneers. It is SO relaxing and nurturing to simply sit down, breathe deeply, look at my plate, and enjoy my meal, period. Nothing more, nothing less.

TIME OF DAY

As modern schedules get more and more hectic, it has become near impossible to create an orderly day centered around meals. The structure of the day is a subtle factor that has been hard for me to discern. I have begun to notice that a more chaotic, or later eating schedule (snacking, skipping meals, eating on the run) creates more susceptibility to tiredness, difficulty with sleep and so called "normal" aches and pains. I know that one of my habits with most negative impact is to eat before sleeping. Those deep sleep night hours are when the system does a whole lot of deep cleaning, from our lungs to intestines to brain to kidneys - the body is rejuvenating like late night janitors preparing for the next active day. If food is clogging up the system, this work cannot be done efficiently. This can also lead to acid reflux and damage to the esophagus. My cleaning organs are working overtime and not getting a whole lot done, so then I'll wake up cranky and tired, worn out after eight hours of sleep.

Eating regularly, at the same time every day preferably earlier in the day, is comforting. This is a form of "giving back" to my organs for the demanding job they do every day, helping to keep those aches and pains away. And, if I can just wait three hours after eating before I lay down, my energy levels vastly improve and my emotions clear up. I wake up refreshed and clear of brain fog. This can make all the difference.

Environment

In many ways the global food system, which has developed to protect people from the ebbs and flows of the seasons, as well as modern buildings which protect people so completely from the elements, have weakened our abilities to cope and adapt. Modern people are often quite stressed out! It is possible that we are not that relaxed living separately from the gathered, daily participation with our local foods and fuel. It can be liberating to head in the opposite direction. Living in a home that experiences natural fluctuations in temperature, eating wild foods growing outside our door, knowing and shopping with our farmers and/or growing as much as we can, syncs our system with our natural environment. This strengthens one's immunity, and gives us a more secure emotional and physical base. This is the way our ancestors ate for countless generations, and it made them strong. Eating more stored roots in the winter time, and fresh greens in the summertime, has an unmistakable energizing effect.

Also, in every environment on earth, city, town, or countryside - surprise! - there are wild, edible plants growing. There are knowledgeable wild foods traditions for each area. Here on the Central Kenai Peninsula of Alaska, there are dandelions, nettles, cucumber shoots, fiddlehead ferns, alaria kelp, yarrow, wild chamomile, mint, birch sap, countless berries and many mushrooms, just to name my favorites. These plants have thrived in our climate for millennia and have innate strength and robust qualities to share that no other foods can provide. It is easy to gather a few each year in season, and integrate as a small percent of one's diet. Even a small amount can lend us vigor and natural immunity stemming from our sense of place.

Moreover, we humans are social creatures and our human environment is a part of who we are. All of our ancestors for thousands of years of human development lived in tight-knit social structures - villages, tribes, extended clans - which were intimately involved with each other, and with the land around them. Only in the past 200 years has technology advanced, and cultures disassembled, to allow people to live "alone". It is not our natural state. It is quite hard to separate out from the culture around you about something as basic as daily meals. The food we eat must resonate with our circle of support for it to be sustainable, and sustain us. Finding like-minded humans, with whom to share our views and food experience, is deeply needed for enduring change.

Creating a collection of people with quiet space in their lives to grow, gather and eat local whole foods is HUGE, comparable to developing renewable, safe sources of energy. The effects are substantial, on a personal and societal level. Mental, physical and social health, as well as environmental stewardship, springs from these practices. Margaret Mead said, "Never doubt that a small committed group of citizens can change the course of history. Indeed, that is the only thing that ever has." I feel that when a small committed group of men, women and children can eat regular, quiet, whole foods meals which were locally grown, it does indeed change the course of history.

Creating all this is the elusively simple practice known as macrobiotics.

MINDS AND SPIRITS

"It's not that I am so smart. But I stay with the questions much longer." ~ Albert Einstein

After raising myself along with a family for the last thirty years out here at Ionia, I sometimes reflect on it all. Our eldest son is writing podcasts in New York City, and our youngest girl is running around with her friends through the mud puddle outside my window. In our home, expressing oneself with a livable tone, and cooking delicious whole foods meals, were always of most importance. Natural foods are still important to my whole brood, and they each continue to cook, no matter what else they are pursuing. I admit, I am proud of that. Half are here in Alaska and half abroad in the world.

My children's home-based education also included listening to Ionia's morning meetings and, eventually, speaking up to contribute their views on every subject under the sun. When my son Connor was seventeen, he began to add his voice to our meetings. One of his first contributions was to suggest that we take away our clocks for a while, to see what life was like without that pressured sense of time. Of course we did it, because the seventeen year olds know best. It revolutionized our days in a tiny, yet noticeable, way. We cooked without timers, and one activity followed another throughout the day without a sense of whether we were late or early. Now that Connor is a bit older, he is exploring the fascinating fervor of fermentation: he leads our explorations into making miso, shoyu, pickles of all kinds, beers and sourdoughs. Here in our little shire, food is often first and foremost in our minds.

At Ionia, we talk about the idea that beliefs, attitudes, emotions and vision are all food, too. Our daily morning meeting is where we use ingredients from the world of spirit, intention and theory to cook up the meals that sustain a community's minds and hearts. Each day, we put our minds together to cook up as whole a picture as we can see, to go along with the whole foods we are eating.

There is no shortage of subjects to look at and we don't shy away from any: multi-generations, parenting, money, competition, sex and relationships, activity and education, stimulants and addiction, religion and politics, energy and farming. The daily conversation changes with the daily pressures and concerns… everything is personal, and everything is universal, at the same time. Often we cook up kind of a tone poem to try to describe What's Going On with as much dimension as we can… Sometimes we laugh at our own absurdities and sometimes we cry with frustration and pressure. Sometimes, on a lazy morning, we just hear someone's reflections about their childhood and dreams of the future. Sometimes, we strongly disagree about issues dear to our hearts, and the thunder crackles. More than once in awhile, the combined wisdom in the room is profound and inspiring, and our collected spirit sparkles like sun on the water. New ideas emerge and take shape, gradually, like weaving a cloth. With natural foods and simple seasonal activities as the backdrop to this conversation, slowly, subtly, common sense comes alive.

The second generation Ionians are surprising in many ways, even to me. They all verbally express themselves beautifully. Some normal, societal American meanings of words have somehow changed along the way… and as the language shifts, so have their attitudes shifted about many cultural norms. They are re-defining what's worth doing, what defines success and family, work versus play. They are, as a group, sensitive and passionate, and relate easily to all ages. Some of these second generational communitarians are very well-read, and some don't read. Some build gorgeous wooden furniture, some make lovely music, and some are intensely interested in fermentation and agriculture. Some of them have left to follow other adventures, while others have settled in to raise their own kids. They all fiercely miss their interconnected extended family when they aren't here. A few have inherited some stormy emotions from their parents, and all have had difficulty adjusting to the more alone and compartmentalized lifestyle of America. The young men and women who are making their lives at Ionia are growing into a gentle force which determines our days and makes many community decisions now. The elders continue to provide our backbone of support, and the combination of generational viewpoints mingle pretty well. In 2002, Ionia built a Longhouse, a large log community center with a large central community kitchen, and that has changed our lives forever. As a mother, most of the pressures of every day cooking, cleaning and childcare are no longer pressing. What an amazing deal! When I cook now, it is often with a team of cooks, and we are serving fifty people. Now that the second generation is having their own children, their daily issues about baby food, teething and diapers swirl around me in familiar echoes of my younger days. The Longhouse is full of crying infants and giggling toddlers.

My initial diehard idealism has mellowed. I have become very patient with our shared back and forth process about food, and all things. It seems that all change moves forward in waves, or spirals. I am challenged by chewing, and excited by quiet meals. I continue to love food.

My cooking skills have also deepened, and I am humbled and energized by the excellent cooks who surround me. Many international influences pass through Ionia's Longhouse kitchen now… Cooks from Japan, Vietnam, Guatemala, Mexico, Italy, Taiwan, India have all shared their wonderful traditional fare with us, and each rubs off a bit into our traditions. Renowned macrobiotic chefs bring their classes here and we all eagerly soak up their knowledge.

Ionians prefer not to work too hard, but somehow we muddle into getting much done together. We're still talking. We're still meeting every morning. We're still having new crops of babies, and more than thirty years later, we're still here. Perhaps some day, we will grow up as a community and Ionia will give birth to baby villages, who, together, will learn to cook up a way of life, without recipes.

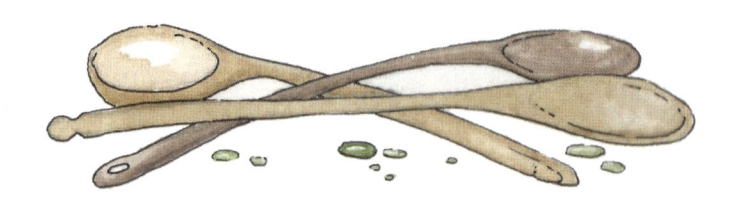

PHOTO SCRAPBOOK

Eliza & Ted get married in San Francisco, October 1981

Elliza with #1 son, John Emrys, July 1982

Eliza, Ted, John & newborn Katie in Boston, December 1983

Eliza with daughters Katie & Jane, Boston 1985

Ionia founding mamas, Kasilof, Alaska 1988

all of the Ionia kids, new cabin construction, 1988

hand laundry in the tipi village, 1988

winter in the tipi, 1988

growing family: Seldovia, Alaska, August 1992

Jane, Alex, Gregs and Katie - In the woods, Kasilof, 1993

Lauden and turnip greens, July 1993

all of the siblings at home, 1995

the Eller Family Home - Wintertime

... and Summertime

birthplace of many Eller babies

Ionia Gardens

grain trials demonstration

drying wild sea vegetables 2013

Connor, Gregory and James, 2005

boys in the Chugach mountains, 2008

Jane and Katie cooking, 2010

Rosalie & Juliet listening to new nephew Hiro, before he is born - Summer 2015

the whole family, August, 2015

14 year old Ellen with her favorite snack (wild blueberries)

8 year old Liam with his favorite snack (garden carrots)

11 year old Aaron with his favorite snack (homemade tofu)

Eliza cooking, 2015

garden harvest, 2013

Ted on the barn, 2014

102

food at Ionia

104

Ionia Today

106

107

Eliza Eller lives on the Kenai Peninsula in Alaska at the village of Ionia (www.ionia.org). She spends her days growing food in the summers and carrying firewood in the winters, soaking in the arctic sun, organizing events and gatherings, keeping in touch with her growing family and scrambling to keep up with the ever moving generations of change at Ionia. She occasionally gets creative with a children's poem book or this cook book. She hangs out around guys who love building with clay and straw, and it is catching, so on a warm Summer day, if she isn't weeding in one if the many greenhouses, one might find her, covered with clay, madly mixing a barrel of slip.

Eliza cooks regularly at the Ionia Longhouse, and for her family. She is learning so much about fermenting from her sons Connor and Gregory and from reading those awesome authors Sandor Katz and Michael Pollan. She is passionate about learning how best to partner with microbes in the soil and in the ferments. Her favorite foods are miso soup, brown rice nori rolls, corn porridge, hiziki salad, and blueberry pear pudding.

To get in touch with Eliza, you can write her at ellers@ionia.org.

Mirra Kohlmoos is an artist and adventurer. Cooking Without Recipes is her first full illustration work but she has also done some commissions. Current projects include adult coloring books. She is a mariner and spends time in the Northeast where she keeps her sail boat. She was raised in rural Wisconsin, with four sisters in a small cabin with no running water, heated by a wood cook stove. Garden food and playing in the woods were her upbringing. Some of Mirra's favorite foods are winter squash, kale, apples and raspberries, as well as fresh snow peas from the vine.

Made in the USA
Middletown, DE
29 August 2019